access to geography

HUMAN GEOGRAPHY – CHANGE *in the* UNITED KINGDOM *in the last* 30 YEARS

David Redfern

Hodde

A MEMBER OF T

Acknowledgements

My thanks are directed towards two areas of my life.

Firstly, in the world of examining I am grateful to Malcolm Skinner, Chair of Examiners at AQA, for his constant encouragement and guidance over the last twenty years, but particularly so for the last ten. It was also his idea (or his fault) that I consider writing this text.

Secondly, I must thank my wife, Tina, and my sons, Michael and Andrew, for their continued support, but in particular for avoiding me during the evenings and weekends when this was written.

David Redfern

Every effort has been made to trace and acknowledge ownership of copyright. The publishers will be glad to make suitable arrangements with any copyright holders whom it has not been possible to contact.

Orders: please contact Bookpoint Ltd, 130 Milton Park, Abingdon, Oxon OX14 4SB. Telephone: (44) 01235 827720. Fax: (44) 01235 400454. Lines are open from 9.00–6.00, Monday to Saturday, with a 24 hour message answering service. Email address: *orders@bookpoint.co.uk*

British Library Cataloguing in Publication Data
A catalogue record for this title is available from the British Library

ISBN 0 340 800305

First Published 2001
Impression number   10 9 8 7 6 5 4 3 2 1
Year   2008 2007 2006 2005 2004 2003 2002

Copyright © 2002 David Redfern

Cover photo shows the Eden project, reproduced courtesy of © Herbie Knott.
Typeset by Fakenham Photosetting Limited Fakenham Norfolk.
Printed in Great Britain for Hodder & Stoughton Education, a division of Hodder Headline Plc, 338 Euston Road, London NW1 3BH by Bath Press Ltd

Contents

Chapter 1   The changing sectoral and spatial organisation
of business   1
1   Introduction   1
2   Changes in manufacturing industry in the
last 30 years   1
Case study: A declining manufacturing industry
– the steel industry in Consett, Durham   5
3   The growth of new manufacturing industries
and new industrial areas   6
Case study: A growing manufacturing area – the
M4 corridor   10
4   Overseas investment and its effects   12
5   Changes in the service industry in the last
30 years   14
6   The changing nature of retailing   18
Case study: A major retailing area – Manchester   21
7   Socio-economic changes in employment   24
Summary   26

Chapter 2   Variations in population age structures over time   28
1   Introduction   29
2   Population structure   29
3   Changes in household composition in the
last 30 years   33
Case study: The Stockbridge Village Trust – an
example of a Housing Association scheme   39
4   The geographical segregation of social groups   42
Summary   51

Chapter 3   Inner cities   55
1   Introduction   55
2   The causes of inner city decline   55
3   Urban regeneration policies   58
Case study: The London Docklands   65
Case study: The Central Manchester
Development Corporation (CMDC)   68
Case study: The Hulme City Challenge
(Manchester)   69
Case study: The Grainger Town Regeneration
Project, Newcastle upon Tyne   69
4   Gentrification   72
5   Making inner cities safer – the female
perspective   73
Summary   75

Chapter 4   Suburbanisation and counter-urbanisation   77
1   Introduction   77

2 Suburbanisation   77
3 Counter-urbanisation   78
Case study: The effects of counter-urbanisation –
St Ives, Cambridgeshire   79
Summary   81

Chapter 5 Managing urban transport   83
1 Introduction   83
2 How and why is traffic increasing?   84
3 Atmospheric pollution in urban areas   85
4 Possible solutions to urban transport problems   85
Case study: Commuting by rail into London   88
Summary   90

References   91

Appendix: Developing extended prose and essay writing skills   92
Index   94

1 The changing sectoral and spatial organisation of business

1 Introduction

This chapter examines the changing nature of business in the UK over the last 30 years. It looks at the decline of the traditional forms of manufacturing industry, the growth of new manufacturing industries, and the major changes in the service industries with particular reference to retailing.

2 Changes in manufacturing industry in the last 30 years

Since the mid-1970s, the UK, in common with other industrialised countries around the world, has seen massive change in manufacturing industry. Some industries have undergone major decline, whereas others have grown markedly. Many of the areas of growth have been stimulated by investment from overseas.

Manufacturing industry has declined in its relative importance both in terms of employment and its contribution to the national economy. Over 7 million people were employed in manufacturing industry in the mid 1970s, whereas by 2000 the number had fallen to 4 million. This progressive decline has been called de-industrialisation.

The following points summarise the main aspects of manufacturing change:

- De-industrialisation has seen the decline of manufacturing industry and has caused job losses and stricken communities once based on traditional manufacturing industries.

- Industrial revival, brought about by both private and public capital, has made an uneven impact, with some areas still suffering from the social and economic effects of industrial closures.
- Industrial revival has been brought about by massive investment from overseas, and by technological developments arising out of research and development institutions. It has not always been successful, particularly that resulting from overseas investment.
- Manufacturing industry now employs fewer workers than the growing tertiary or service based industries.
- Non traditionally manufacturing areas of the UK have gained manufacturing jobs more rapidly than urban areas.
- The use of high technology in manufacturing processes has created its own requirements for industrial location, and has had a significant effect on working practices within the industry.
- Sensitivity towards the environment, both locally and nationally, now has a major influence in decision-making.

a) The decline of the traditional forms of manufacturing industry

The main manufacturing industries which have declined in the last 30 years are those which were established in the nineteenth and early twentieth century. Their growth was based on the use of coal and imported raw materials, such as iron ore and cotton. A key aspect of their development was the ability to export the finished products to other countries around the world, particularly former colonial countries. Consequently, the major industrial areas were either on the major coalfields or at coastal ports located on deep water estuaries (Figure 1).

Examples of such industries include:

- Textiles: woollen cloth in West Yorkshire (Leeds, Bradford, Huddersfield); cotton cloth in Lancashire (Bolton, Bury, Burnley).
- Steel in Sheffield, Middlesbrough and North and South Wales.
- Shipbuilding in Newcastle, Sunderland, Belfast and Glasgow.
- Chemicals in the North East (Middlesbrough) and the North West (Widnes and Runcorn).
- The car industry and component suppliers in Birmingham, other parts of the West Midlands and Luton.
- Clothing, food processing, and other port industries in the East End of London.
- Pottery and other household goods in the area around Stoke.

The reasons for the decline of these industries are many, some due to changes within the UK, some due to factors taking place elsewhere in the world:

1. There has been an increased use of mechanisation, such as automation, robotics and computerised production lines. These have reduced the

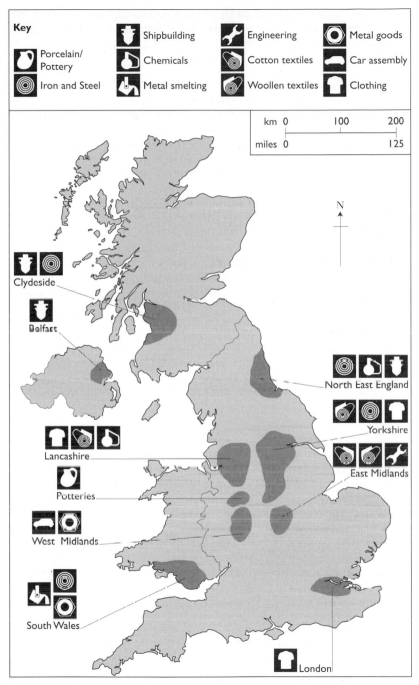

Figure 1 Traditional industrial areas in the UK

number of workers needed for the manufacturing process, so it has become less labour intensive. The original tasks undertaken by unskilled and semi-skilled labour have been the easiest to replace by mechanisation.

2. There has been a loss of competitiveness, which has caused UK industry to lose many of its overseas markets, as well as its home market. Competition from overseas, particularly from the newly industrialised countries (NICs) of the Pacific Rim (Hong Kong, Singapore, Taiwan, South Korea) severely disadvantaged UK industry. In the Pacific Rim countries, production costs were significantly reduced mainly due to lower labour costs. In addition, much of the manufacturing industry in the UK had outdated buildings, and inefficient equipment, both of which added to production costs.

3. Working practices within the UK were traditional. They involved the division of labour, the breaking down of a task into small repetitive fragments, each of which could be done at speed by workers with little specialist training. Such practices were characteristic of mass production assembly lines which produced standardised products. The newer industrial areas began to develop working practices which could be more flexible, both in terms of production but also in terms of the use of machinery and labour. The latter resulted in multi-tasking i.e. one worker being able to do several jobs.

4. There was a world economic recession in the early 1980s, and at this time the value of sterling rose. This had a dual effect, the cost of UK manufactured goods rose at a time when worldwide demand was falling. The Conservative Government at that time believed that manufacturing industry should strive to become competitive and not be protected by government assistance. A number of industries, some formerly owned by the government such as British Steel, were forced to 'go it alone' and were privatised. Subsidies and other support mechanisms were dropped. Rationalisation took place whereby production was concentrated in a smaller number of highly mechanised units so as to remain competitive. Uncompetitive industries closed. In most cases, rationalisation meant redundancy.

5. Political factors were also of importance during the long period of manufacturing decline under the Conservative Government from 1979 to 1997. The government demanded a less unionised labour force, particularly in the mining and manufacturing industries, and strived to 'defeat' many of the trade unions. The Conservative Party had previously suffered at the hands of some of the trade unions in the coal mining and motor vehicle industries.

6. During the latter part of the 1990s and the early part of the twenty-first century, the problems of global overcapacity that once appeared in the iron and steel industry and shipbuilding, have reappeared in the motor vehicle industry. The two 'giants' of the industry, Ford and General Motors, have decided to cease car assembly at Dagenham and Luton respectively due to falling demand for cars in Europe. Spare capacity

cannot exist in the global strategies of these two firms, and there are worries that this will affect other manufacturers in years to come, particularly as the major players in the industry continue to merge to share design and production costs.

Finally, despite the above concerns for manufacturing industry in the UK, the overall output of manufacturing industry has increased. This has been due to the expansion of new factories manufacturing motor vehicles, computers and related equipment, and other electrical goods. De-industrialisation has been selective, both in terms of the industries and the areas affected.

Case study: A declining manufacturing industry – the steel industry in Consett, Durham

In the mid 1960s the British Steel Corporation had a workforce of 250,000, producing nearly 25 million tonnes of steel at 23 locations. In the mid 1990s British Steel had reduced its workforce to 55,000, with a production of 14 million tonnes at just 4 locations.

This reduction was caused by huge overcapacity around the world, with new steel making facilities appearing in places such as India, South Korea and Taiwan. The response of the European nations was to rationalise production. Many high cost inland locations were closed, such as at Bilston in the West Midlands and Consett in north east England. Only the biggest and most efficient integrated works (Redcar-Lackenby, Scunthorpe, Llanwern and Port Talbot) survived in the UK. British Steel has subsequently merged with the Dutch company Hoogovens to form Corus, and this company announced the closure of Llanwern as a steel making plant in February 2001.

Steel works are very much dependent on ease of transport of raw materials. They need access to wide deep sheltered estuaries through which coal and iron ore are imported from countries such as Australia, Brazil and Liberia. These same ports can be used for exporting the finished steel, as well as using railways to access home markets.

Consett began as a steel making town in 1840, based around local deposits of coking coal and blackband iron ore. By the late 1880s the furnaces at Consett were producing 10% of the nation's steel. A town grew up around the steel works, which meant that most of the houses and shops were owned by the steel company.

In 1980, the closure of Consett was announced on economic grounds. Production was to be transferred to the more cost efficient works on the coast at Redcar-Lackenby. The local raw materials had long since been exhausted, and financial losses were high due to the small capacity of the works. The main market for the Consett plant, shipbuilding on the Rivers Tyne and Wear and at Barrow in Furness, had also largely closed down. Closure resulted in the immediate loss of 4000 jobs, and the town faced economic disaster. Male unemployment in the town was set to rise to 30%, adding to the unemployment caused by the decline of the surrounding coal industry. This was exacerbated by the subsequent closure of another large industry – a ball-bearing manufacturer.

However, Consett did not die as a town. Shortly after the closure of the steel works a number of organisations (private businesses, local government agencies and the local authority) set up the Derwentside Industrial Development Agency. This encouraged a number of companies to move into the area, the most famous of which were Derwent Valley Foods (makers of Phileas Fogg snacks) which employs 80 people, and Blue Ridge Care, a manufacturer of disposable nappies. Over 200 companies, some computer based, have been established in new purpose-built units, creating over 3500 jobs in total. These companies were encouraged by grants and loans, and also by the substantial improvements made to the local environment, such as the greening over and landscaping of the spoil tips.

The area's economy has diversified and strengthened, but it still remains weak in comparison to the UK generally. One of the main problems that still remains is a low educational attainment. This is below both regional and national levels, with 18% and 40% of the adults having low levels of literacy and numeracy respectively. Similarly, there are low attainment levels in both GCSE and GCE performances, 25% and 31% below national levels respectively.

In terms of retail trade, Consett town centre continues to do well. There is a lower level of vacant floorspace than the national average, although investigations into shopping habits reveal a dominance of convenience expenditure over comparison goods expenditure. This is probably due to the proximity of major retail areas in Durham and the Metro Centre in Gateshead.

3 The growth of new manufacturing industries and new industrial areas

The majority of new manufacturing industries in the last 10–20 years have been high technology industries, such as computers and computer related equipment, telecommunications and micro-electronics.

In addition, many of the traditional industries have advanced by adopting new technologies and working practices, for example, the car assembly industry. A key feature of these types of industries is the importance of Research and Development. This is needed to develop new products and modify existing products, as well as keeping 'ahead of the game' in terms of product design.

For these 'new' industries, a highly skilled and qualified workforce is essential, and access to raw materials is less important. Consequently, such industry has become concentrated in areas where either the workforce can be attracted or is available, or where the government wants to encourage it to locate. A term often used in connection with these industries is that they are *footloose*. Another name that is commonly attached to them is that of being *sunrise* industries, because of their general growth. Common elements of their location at a local scale include being on new industrial estates on the edges of towns, or alongside motorways to utilise an efficient transport system.

The following are the main areas of new industrial growth:

- 'Silicon Glen' in central Scotland
- the Cambridge area, and along the M11
- the 'Sunrise Strip' of the M4 corridor
- 'Honda' Valley, South Wales, and the Honda assembly plant at Swindon
- new car assembly plants in the North East (Washington), and East Midlands (Burnaston)
- many small light industrial estates in rural areas such as East Anglia, and Sussex.

The reasons for these changes are many, reflecting changes both within the UK, and economic changes taking place around the world:

1. There has been massive inward investment by overseas transnational companies (TNCs), for example by Japanese, South Korean and German firms. In the case of the motor vehicle industry a number of Japanese car manufacturers have come to the UK and built huge new plants, the three largest being Nissan, Toyota and Honda. Nissan was the first. It began production in 1986 with an initial output of 100,000 cars per year, rising to over 270,000 in 1993. Their factory at Washington New Town in the north east of England was the largest single investment by a Japanese company in Europe. Other similar investments followed at Burnaston in north Derbyshire where a large Toyota plant was built next to the A38 trunk road, and Honda assembly plant at Swindon on the M4. Further inward investment followed in other parts of the UK, although this has not always been as successful. The examples of the Fujitsu (Japan) and Samsung (South Korean) investments which have both been subsequently closed down illustrate this.

2. The development of numerous motorways and airports for ease of communication has been a major factor. In these industries, speed of access is important both for people, and for raw materials and products.

3. Proximity to universities with expertise and research facilities, and also to recruit highly skilled/intelligent labour has been of major significance. The first and biggest Science Park in the UK was the Cambridge Science Park, located on the northern edge of this famous university city (Figure 2). There are well over 700 hi-tech companies within the Cambridge region (known as 'Silicon Fen') which employ over 20,000 people. Its growth is clearly linked to the nearby university where a pool of highly educated and technologically qualified workers and scientists exists. These have generated high personal incomes with which entre-preneurship has developed even further. Research and Development opportunities are encouraged by the university. The building of the M11 has also acted as a growth factor. In 1999 an additional boost came when Microsoft chose Cambridge as the centre of its European operations and pledged £50 million to build its first European computer research centre there. This will encourage further companies to move into the area, keen to take advantage of the 'synergy' that will develop. Synergy is the intense localised interaction between different firms (research organis-ations, banks, entrepreneurs, service organisations) on the same site which creates benefits for all of the participants.

4. To many of these new industries, an attractive environment is a very important locational factor. Many business and science parks have been built on greenfield sites where the relative low cost of land has been an advantage. The high quality of the environment is thought to assist in the creative development that is required by such industries.

5. Aid packages from various levels of government (local and national), or from government sponsored bodies, have encouraged overseas and home investment in certain areas of the UK. The revival of old industrial areas and the industrialisation of new areas has been a focus for most gov-ernments in the last 30 years, but with a varying degree of commitment. A wide variety of regional policies have been set up in an attempt to redress imbalances of economic and social development. These have included:

   - **Assisted Areas** – carefully defined parts of the UK in which gov-ernment grants may be given to persuade firms to locate there. At various times in the last 30 years these have been named as Special Development areas, Development Areas, and Intermediate Areas with varying levels of incentives being offered.
   - **Enterprise Zones** – areas at a more local scale set up to attract industry by the removal of certain taxes (local and national) and local authority planning controls. Typical enterprise zones were small, 100–200 hectares in size, sometimes built on greenfield sites, and sometimes on areas within inner cities with 'development potential' (often a euphemism for empty and derelict).
   - **Urban Development Corporations** and other urban regenera-tion schemes which are examined later in this book.

6. The growth of these new industries has allowed the transfer of tech-nology to the UK. This is the movement of new working practices and other innovations into the country. These include:

1 Aston Science Park
2 Brunel Science Park
3 Cambridge Science Park
4 Cefn Llan Science and Technology Park
5 Chilworth Research Centre
6 Co-operative Education Centre
7 University of Durham Industrial Research Laboratories
8 University of East Anglia Industrial Liaison Unit
9 University College Galway Industrial Liaison Office
10 Heriot Watt Research Park, Edingburgh
11 Keele University Science Park
12 Listerhills High Technology Development
13 Liverpool University R&D Advisory Unit
14 Loughborough Technology Centre

15 Manchester University/ Manchester Science Park
16 Merseyside Innovation Centre
17 St Johns Innovation Park, Cambridge
18 Surrey University/ Surrey Research Park
19 University of Warwick Science Park
20 Scottish Developement Agency and Universities of Glasgow, Strathclyde, and West of Scotland Science Park
21 Applied Statistics Research Unit, University of Kent, Canterbury
22 Stirling University Innovation Park
23 St Andrews Technology Centre
24 Dundee Technology Park
25 Aberdeen Science and Research Park

Figure 2 Science research parks in the British Isles

- The JIT (Just in Time) system of production. This is a manufacturing system designed to minimise the costs of holding stocks of raw materials and components by carefully planned scheduling and flow of resources through the production process. It requires a very efficient ordering system and reliability of delivery. It was introduced to the UK by the car manufacturers such as Nissan. In this case there is hourly delivery of some parts, and many component manufacturers have been forced to relocate close to the assembly plant. Another requirement of the JIT system is that there must be zero defect and total quality control. Hence, car manufacturers have very close and strong links with their suppliers, which are monitored rigorously.
- Teams of flexible multi-tasking workers who rotate jobs, helping to increase skill levels. Again in the case of car assembly, production can be more tailored to the needs of the individual customer. Standardised products are fewer, with a greater range of specialised products being made. It also allows more flexible production which can meet even the smallest alteration in market demand at short notice.

Case study: A growing manufacturing area – the M4 Corridor

The M4 Corridor (shown on Figure 3) lies to the west of London and follows the route of the M4 motorway towards Reading, Newbury, Swindon and Bristol into South Wales. Many high technology industries have located here including information technology industries, computer based industries, telecommunications and micro electronics. Research and Development sites are also widespread, some related to private industries and others related to government institutions.

A number of advantages are possessed by this area:

- The proximity of the M4 (from West to East) and the A34 (from North to South) have aided communication by road.
- The electrified railway out of Paddington has also assisted in terms of transport of key workers to business meetings in London.
- The presence of Heathrow airport to the west of London has allowed easy access for both visiting businessmen and salesmen going abroad.
- The previous location of government research centres (Aldermaston and Harwell) have encouraged related industries to locate in the same area.
- The booming inward migration of people from the rest of the UK into the area to seek highly paid employment has provided a skilled and motivated workforce.
- The proximity to universities, such as Oxford and Reading, has

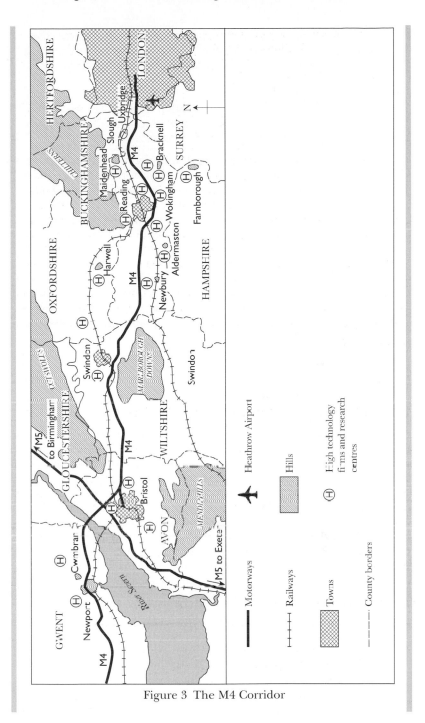

Figure 3 The M4 Corridor

stimulated research projects and encouraged further development of expertise. Science and Business Parks have become established right across the area encouraging synergy and the exchange of ideas and information.
- The attractive environment of the Thames Valley, together with other areas such as the Cotswolds, Mendips, Chilterns and Marlborough Downs all provide potential locations for homes for the highly paid key workers in these industries.

Swindon lies halfway between London and Bristol, and owes its origin to the railway line between London and South Wales. It was the engineering centre of the Great Western Railway. Today it has attracted, like the rest of the Corridor, a wide range of high technology industries such as Intel, a leading micro-processing company. Manufacturing industry has reduced its share of the employment structure in Swindon (as it has in every other UK town), and the nature of that manufacturing industry has significantly changed. An indication of the increasing wealth of Swindon is the fact that major service industries have moved their administrative headquarters into the town – the insurers Allied Dunbar and Commercial Union, and the Nationwide Building Society.

4 Overseas investment and its effects

Overseas investment is the capital attracted to a region from beyond its boundaries. The UK has attracted such inward investment from a number of countries, such as Japan, South Korea, the USA and other European countries. The main effect has been to create new industries in many areas of the UK. Some of the better known investments include car assembly plants such as Nissan at Washington and Toyota at Burnaston. Other areas of major overseas investment have been in the Central Valley of Scotland, known as 'Silicon Glen' where transnationals based in the USA (e.g. Hewlett Packard) and Japan (e.g. Panasonic) have made large investments.

a) Who benefits from such investments?

The investors themselves benefit for the following reasons:
- There is access to relatively cheap, highly skilled labour. Rates of pay in the UK are below the European average, and are thus a major consideration for any potential investor.
- There are limited financial controls on profit. The UK governments (both Conservative and Labour) have become increasingly business

friendly, and are keen to allow foreign transnationals fair systems of profit management.
* Incentives are provided for peripheral economic areas.
* There is good access to European markets. The European Union alone has a total potential market of 350 million people, many of which have high personal incomes. This is very attractive to new investors from overseas who can foresee huge growth in sales. This does not include the additional potential market now emerging in eastern Europe and the new states of the former Soviet Union.
* European Union regulations now stipulate that a proportion of the finished product of an industry has to be manufactured within the countries of the European Union. This has forced many transnationals, particularly those from the Newly Industrialised Countries of the Pacific Rim to support local component suppliers, or to encourage branches of their home-based component suppliers to re-locate in Britain.
* The UK has a good quality of environment, with attractive scenery and a strong historical legacy. Even the excellence of UK golf courses are cited as being key factors in influencing foreign investors.

Governments (national and local) benefit for the following reasons:

* The inward investment of a transnational replaces the shrinking traditional manufacturing base of a region, thus stimulating regional regeneration.
* It creates a multiplier effect locally. Personal incomes in the vicinity of the investment are increased, there is more spending on local goods and services, and the general wealth and level of infrastructure investment increases.
* The export base of the country is strengthened, improving the balance of trade. Exports of manufactured goods increase in value and amount, enabling a more balanced relationship with imports. This has allowed some repayment of international debt to take place in recent years.
* It results in effective transfer of technology and product development.
* For national government, a clear benefit is the reduction in unemployment related benefits to former workers and their dependents.

Unemployed people in the area of investment benefit for the following reasons:

* Jobs are created. Each investment by an overseas company creates employment in an area. Individual firms create a minimum number of jobs which are added to by component suppliers, subcontractors, service companies, transport, hotels and catering. An investment by one major transnational stimulates further employment growth.
* Living standards are raised. As stated earlier, personal incomes increase as a result of the generation of wealth from employment.

b) Who loses from such investments?

The investment into an area of a major foreign investor does not always have a beneficial effect, either to the local area or the country as a whole. Some of these issues are examined below:

- Transnationals may decide to leave an area once initial aid packages no longer apply. This has been the case in the north east of England where factories owned by Fujitsu and Siemens have closed down. The latter was in receipt of a very large subsidy on arrival, which appeared to have little long term effect.
- Home based industries which produce similar products to those produced by overseas investors have come under increased competition, both in terms of relative costs and product design. The motor vehicle industry illustrates this well, particularly with the overcapacity of car production within the country. This forced the sale of the Rover Group by the Germany based car manufacturer BMW. Rover was subject to a management buy-out and is still producing cars. However, it is clear that the inroads into market shares caused by the arrival of both Toyota and Nissan have been key factors in its demise.
- Wages are sometimes lower than would be the case with domestic industries. Much of the employment created is part-time, female orientated with high annual turnover rates of staff.
- It is said that the work consists merely of screw-driver jobs, with low skill development and few long term career prospects. Many of the managerial positions within the companies are 'imported' into a region, either from abroad or from other parts of the UK.
- The local area often has to bear the costs of training. Local Training and Enterprise Councils (TECs) and local governments are frequently contracted to cover the costs of training and retraining of former employees of traditional industries.

5 Changes in the service industry in the last 30 years

In the 1990s over 70% of the UK workforce was employed in the service sector. Employment in this sector can be divided into three groups, the *producer services, consumer services,* and *public services.*

- **Producer services** exist to serve other organisations, for example a computer consultancy will advise other organisations on the most suitable computer system for their accounting. Similarly, a bank will provide a range of financial services to manufacturing industry. It is now common for many organisations, of varying sizes, to subcontract out services that used to be part of the larger organisation.

- **Consumer services** are provided by retailers, hotels and leisure organisations.
- **Public services** provide for the producer and the consumer. They include provision for social needs (e.g. health, education and social services), infrastructure needs (e.g. road building, railway services), administration of local and national governments, regulation of public and private conduct (e.g. monitoring of environmental pollution or flood levels), and the provision of national security (e.g. the armed forces).

As in manufacturing industry, the onset of rapid technological change is having a major effect on service industries, to the point that it is becoming increasingly difficult to distinguish easily between manufacturing and service industries. In an economic environment increasingly dominated by computers, global communications and companies which are constantly investing in Research and Development, the categorisation of industry is becoming more difficult. Computer based industries which can be found on a Science Park may make computers (manufacturing), but will also distribute them, maintain them and seek to update them (service industry). Some have categorised this type of industry as quaternary, even quinary. What follows is an examination of the key aspects of the 'traditional' service industries as described above.

Service sector employment has increased in all areas of the UK, but concentrations tend to be more notable in:

- London – 5.5% of the UK workforce is located within central London, the vast majority of which works in service related activity. This is one of the world's main centres for finance, business and commerce. Employment has fallen slightly in recent years, mainly as some firms have relocated to other areas in the south east of England.
- The south east of England – predominantly in business and finance.
- The south west of England – largely based around tourism and the leisure industry.
- East Anglia – with significant growth in transport and communications, and social services.

a) The financial service industry of the City of London

The great majority of office space in the City of London is given over to financial, legal and accountancy based activity. The causes of this concentration are largely historical – central London has always been a key financial player in world economics. This has been increased by the globalisation of services, and the need for international banking, accountancy and legal services.

Continued growth may cause some problems:

- There is a difficulty in providing a supply of a highly qualified and technologically skilled workforce.

- There are difficulties in providing and extending suitable office space as the costs per unit area of land are among the highest in the world.
- Devising and introducing improvements in public transport systems that can cope with the influx of workers into the central area.

b) Service growth on the south coast of England

Another feature of the increase in service industries is that coastal resorts which have traditionally provided leisure and recreation facilities, have expanded into other service activities. Bournemouth, for example, becomes a major conference centre during the winter. It has also had a rapid expansion of its office-based employment, with the national headquarters of five companies coming to the town, including Abbey Life and Chase Manhattan Bank. The Chase Manhattan Bank has built a new purpose-designed operation on the outskirts of the town. Over 1000 jobs have been created, half of which were relocated from London. New housing areas have been built, with a subsequent increase in local purchasing power. The company is seeking to expand its offices in the town, and has received planning permission to do so. Bournemouth is now the fifth most important financial centre in the country.

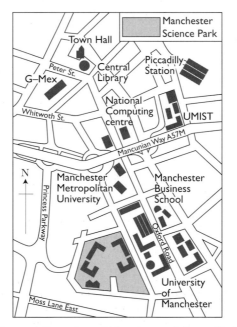

Figure 4 Location of Manchester Science Park

c) The Manchester Science Park

The Manchester Science Park (MSP) is located close to the University of Manchester, but also has close links with other academic institutions in the Manchester area. These include the University of Manchester Institute of Science and Technology (UMIST) and Salford University (Figure 4). Hence the Park aims to link university research closely with high technology companies.

The MSP can be found in landscaped surroundings which were originally used for another industrial purpose. This is an example of a brownfield location which is now an attractive site for employees. It offers new employment opportunities in medical and computer based technology, and makes use of fibre optic links to the nearby university computers. It also has access to the University's library, conference and sports facilities.

d) The tourist industry in Cornwall

The tourist industry is by far the dominant industry in Cornwall. Over 4 million people visit Cornwall each year spending over £900 million. As Cornwall has a remote location, most visitors stay for periods of a week or more which adds greatly to the economic wealth of the county. Over 30,000 people are employed in the industry with many more during the peak of the tourist season. However, much of the investment originates from outside the county, so only about one-third of tourist spending is retained within the Cornwall.

Much of the industry operates at low wage rates, and over time these have continued to fall behind national rates. For men the short-fall is as great as 25%, whereas for women it is 20%. Many of the jobs in tourism and in food and catering are semi or unskilled. In addition much of the work is seasonal, with a significant fall in business between September and March. Unemployment rates increase during the winter months, the rates are usually 2% less in July than in January, and are typically 2–3% higher overall when compared with the rest of the UK.

The accommodation and catering section of the tourist industry illustrates some of the major developments in it. The majority of such trade is concentrated on the coast at resorts such as Newquay, Falmouth and Penzance. However, there are local concentrations at some inland tourist sites, such as near the Lost Gardens of Heligan (which attracts 10,000 people per week in summer) and the River Camel trail. The industry is expanding and taking advantage of natural and human advantages. In August 1999 visitors brought in an additional £50 million due to the solar eclipse. Self-catering and holiday home type holidays are expanding, especially out-of-season. The publicity given to Padstow on a television cookery programme has also seen an increase in the number of visitors to that seaside town.

The Eden Project is another feature on the tourist landscape which will ensure that Cornwall remains a major attraction.

6 The changing nature of retailing

The traditional pattern of retailing is based on two key factors:

- Easy access to goods purchased on a regular basis. These goods include bread, milk and newspapers, and are often called convenience goods.
- People's willingness to travel to a shopping centre for goods with a higher value which are purchased less often. These include household and electrical goods, clothes and shoes, and are often called comparison goods.

For many years, these factors led to a two-tier structure of retailing. Local needs were met by corner shops in terraced housing areas, and by suburban shopping parades along the side of a main road through a residential area. The higher value goods were purchased in the town centre, the Central Business District (CBD), which meant that a trip by bus or car was necessary. However, as in the other industries considered in this book, technology (in the form of the motor vehicle and electronic systems) has had a major influence in changing the patterns of retailing in the last 30 years.

Some of the key developments are given below:

- The 1970s saw the beginning of supermarkets and superstores within residential areas and town centres. In these stores a full range of food and non-food items were sold, with both brand names and shop brands being sold at the same check out desk. This then expanded into a larger version of such establishments called hypermarkets which also sold electrical goods and clothing and often had smaller specialist retail outlets under the same roof. An important factor in the use of these establishments is the use of the private car to load up once or twice a week with 'the family shop'.
- The 1980s saw the expansion of non-food retail parks which concentrated on DIY, carpets and furniture. Many of these were constructed on the outskirts of a town or city, with easy access to main roads, again to attract the car user. The buildings were of a warehouse type construction, often uniform in design, each one being distinguished by the display on the outside and by the internal design.
- The 1990s has seen the growth of huge out-of-town shopping centres on the periphery of major urban areas and close to major motorways. Indeed, they often have their own motorway access and junction points integral to their design. Some of the best known shopping areas in the country are included in this category – The Metro Centre (near Newcastle), Meadowhall (near Sheffield), The Trafford Centre (near Manchester), and Bluewater and Lakeside on either side of the Thames, east of London (Figure 5).

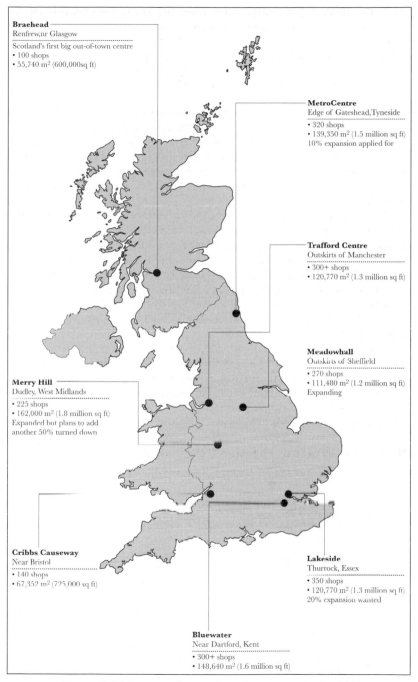

Braehead
Renfrew, nr Glasgow
Scotland's first big out-of-town centre
• 100 shops
• 55,740 m² (600,000 sq ft)

MetroCentre
Edge of Gateshead, Tyneside
• 320 shops
• 139,350 m² (1.5 million sq ft)
10% expansion applied for

Trafford Centre
Outskirts of Manchester
• 300+ shops
• 120,770 m² (1.3 million sq ft)

Meadowhall
Outskirts of Sheffield
• 270 shops
• 111,480 m² (1.2 million sq ft)
Expanding

Merry Hill
Dudley, West Midlands
• 225 shops
• 162,000 m² (1.8 million sq ft)
Expanded but plans to add
another 50% turned down

Cribbs Causeway
Near Bristol
• 140 shops
• 67,352 m² (725,000 sq ft)

Lakeside
Thurrock, Essex
• 350 shops
• 120,770 m² (1.3 million sq ft)
20% expansion wanted

Bluewater
Near Dartford, Kent
• 300+ shops
• 148,640 m² (1.6 million sq ft)

Figure 5 Major out-of-town shopping centres in the UK

During each of these phases of retail change, the traditional town centre has continued to exist. There have been several times when town centre retailing has been said to be dying, and it is certainly the case that in some small towns there has been a general decline. However, many town centres still flourish in addition to the new out-of-town centres. In some cases, the CBD has slowly moved in one or more directions. In other cases new indoor shopping areas or malls have been constructed; for example the Eldon Centre in Newcastle. Another common feature has been the pedestrianisation of many town centres, and the gentrification of shopping areas, as in the case of Brindley Place in Birmingham. Shopping areas are being made more attractive by creating a village type atmosphere, with a mixture of shops, eating places and artistic street furniture to breathe new life into them.

The twenty-first century is beginning to experience e-commerce with electronic home shopping using digital and cable television systems. The impact of this form of retailing on other types of shops has yet to be seen. However, one feature that is already beginning to emerge is that this type of shopping is unlikely to seriously affect existing locations for shopping. People still want to examine items before purchase, and e-commerce will still depend upon mail delivery services, both road and rail based, neither of which can guarantee next day delivery.

Another recent and more localised shopping feature is the increase of the local garage shop. This is again clearly linked to the rise in private car ownership. Local garages are no longer the place people go to get fuel. They can buy newspapers, bread, vegetables, fast food, lottery tickets, and obtain money from a cash machine. The local garage has become the corner shop of the twenty-first century.

a) Factors affecting the changing nature of retailing

A number of factors have combined to produce the above changes in retailing.

1. **The increased mobility allowed by the motor vehicle:** Nearly all of the changes described earlier are due to the increased ownership of the private car and its use. These range from the increased use of the local garage to the large out-of-town shopping areas. Car parking is still expensive and relatively restricted in city centres. Access into such areas is by means of congested roads. Out-of-town retail areas offer large free areas of car parking. Locations next to motorway junctions offer speedy access, and are therefore less stressful. Even at a local level, it is often easier to pull into a garage forecourt to make a low level purchase than to find a parking space outside a suburban shopping parade.

2. **The changing nature of shopping habits:** People now purchase many items as part of a weekly, fortnightly or even monthly shop. The introduction of freezers on a large scale has allowed items which used to be

purchased regularly to be stored for longer periods of time. This has dovetailed with the changing nature of employment. In many cases, either both the income earners or the sole income earner in a family cannot find the time to shop on a daily basis. Retailers have responded to this demand by developing more 'ready made meal' type products which can be stored simply in a domestic freezer.

3. **The changing expectations of shopping habits:** More and more people use shopping as a family social activity, one which can involve more that just the act of shopping. Consequently, many of the larger shopping areas combine retailers with cinemas, restaurants, fast food outlets, crèches and entertainment areas for children. For example the White Rose Centre near Leeds has an area set aside for men who accompany their partners but do not wish to 'shop until they drop'! Such marketing ploys are used to make the customer feel much more at home.

4. **The changing nature of the retailing industry:** There are only a few supermarket/hypermarket companies, each of which strive to be more competitive than the others. They seek to build on cheaper out-of-town locations and to reduce their economies of scale. In this way they can afford to reduce their prices, offer 24-hour shopping and provide large car parking areas.

5. **The changing attitudes of national and local politicians and planners:** The attitudes of politicians is that retail development in out-of-town locations has gone far enough. New life has to be injected into existing CBDs to avoid the problems of economic decline in these areas. Similarly, traffic congestion in out-of-town locations has to be reduced. A number of the major shopping areas identified above have sought permission to expand, and in most cases have been refused. Some supermarket chains are turning their attention back into their existing and new CBD outlets. For example, J Sainsbury have developed new 'local' stores which do not sell the full range of goods found in their larger outlets, but do stock items targeted at local needs.

Case study: A major retailing area – Manchester

Manchester's CBD is identified in Figure 6. It is the area where the city's shops, financial centres and offices are located. This important area is bounded by a motorway, inner ring road and railway stations. The high density of streets reflects two features, the historical core of the city and the high land values of the buildings that exist there.

The sale of products or services requires customers. If customers know where to come for that service and can reach it easily, then there is a greater chance of a sale. The CBD is traditionally the most accessible area of a town or city because it is in the centre. It is also that part of the city where property is most

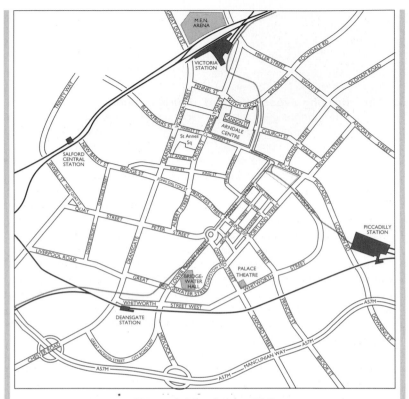

Figure 6 Manchester CBD

in demand from which sales can be achieved. High prices or land values therefore result from companies seeking land in this small accessible space.

Manchester has a network of roads which lead to and radiate from the CBD. The city is also encircled by a new ring motorway – the M60 – but it also has two motorways which come very close into the city centre, the M602 and the A57 (M). In addition, the city is served by two main-line railway stations, Piccadilly and Victoria, which link it to the rest of the UK. Railway stations serving the local area are also found on the edge of the CBD – Deansgate and Oxford Road. The city is also served by the light-rail system of the Metrolink bringing shoppers into the city from Bury to the north and Altrincham to the south.

As in most CBDs, similar functions in Manchester often locate together, or cluster, as they are competing for the same customers. Frequent clusters include:

- Retail outlets such as department stores, shoe shops and clothing shops, as along Market Street.
- Office functions such as those involved in the sale of property, namely estate agents, banks and building societies, solicitors and insurance companies, as in the George Street area.
- Chinese restaurants as in the Chinatown area of Princess Street and Faulkner Street.
- Nightclubs and other places of entertainment, where several venues may be located in the same area of the CBD, such as around the Palace Theatre and Bridgewater Hall.

Another feature developing in Manchester is the division in functions according to social background and income. It is increasingly being recognised that people of differing social bases tend to make use of quite different parts of the city centre. In Manchester, lower income people are found more frequently in Oldham Road and the markets area of the city where there is a higher concentration of bargain and discount shops. Conversely, the area around St Ann's Square and King Street has a higher proportion of young professional people with outlets such as wine bars and designer shops being more common.

The Trafford Centre

When the Trafford Centre was opened in 1998 many people were concerned about the effect it would have on the CBD of Manchester. Nearly 5.4 million people (almost 10% of the UK population) live within 45 minutes drive time of the centre. It was designed to be more than just a shopping centre, with a 1600 seat food court, an 18 lane ten-pin bowling alley and a 20 screen cinema. The Trafford Centre offers the following advantages:

- 10,000 free car parking spaces.
- Facilities for the disabled which are regularly spaced within the complex. These include a Shop Mobility Unit offering scooters and wheelchairs.
- A weatherproof air conditioned and safe environment.
- Its own security system, with a tannoy system, and a meeting point for lost children.
- A full range of peripheral services, such as a post office, banks and travel agents.

Typical of similar out-of-town retail areas, it also has a range of disadvantages:

- Heavy build-up of traffic on the access road network takes place at certain times of the year, such as Christmas and Bank Holidays.
- The atmosphere within the complex is artificial. There are a

number of themed sections which reflect the styles of Italy, China Town and New Orleans.

- All of the stores are national chain stores – it is difficult for local businesses to become established.
- Access is restricted to those who can get there, usually by car. In 1999, 85% of the visitors came by car. Public transport facilities are limited, which makes it difficult for the elderly in particular to go there. However, there are plans to provide a Metrolink connection to the centre, as well as a rail link.

Manchester as a leisure area

Manchester offers a wide range of entertainment and leisure related activities. In addition to the usual city centre pubs and restaurants, there are other experiences such as opera, theatre, classical music and ballet. Nationally well known venues include the Bridgewater Hall, the Cornerhouse Cinema complex, Granada Studios, the Museum of Science and Industry and the roman site at Castlefields. One of the main reasons for the increased use of Manchester as a leisure base, particularly in the evening, is the increased use of CCTV. This is also having a beneficial effect on shopping, making the environment more safe and crime free.

7 Socio-economic changes in employment

The growth of service industries in particular has had a significant effect on employment patterns. These include:

- **Gender differences**: Larger numbers of females are employed in many industries, often making use of flexible working hours, and part-time work. 'Flexitime' is now a common feature of the service industries. This means that firms and organisations can respond easily and cheaply to fluctuations in demand, for example, when there is Christmas shopping at supermarkets and other retail outlets, and in hotels in the summer.
  Some services are becoming increasingly female dominant, for example catering and hotel work, teaching and work in science and business parks. Extra security systems are being put in place by many such firms to enable female staff to come and go at night. In some service industries, males are beginning to take on what were traditionally regarded as 'female roles', for example cleaning services and nursing.
- **Worksharing** is also a feature of many service industries. This entails two people sharing the one job between them. This is ideally suited to

mothers who wish to retain some working life and the income that goes with it, as well as being at home to bring up a young child. There are some industries where this is easier to achieve than others. Those that require continuity of inter-personal relationships, such as doctors and teachers, find that worksharing is more difficult to develop successfully than in office based clerical tasks.

*   **Homeworking and teleworking** are also increasing with the widespread use of the telephone, the Internet, and video-conferencing. This involves a worker being largely based at home, and working using computer technology. Typical industries making use of this include design based work, journalism, advertising and call centre work. In the case of design technology, both the design brief and the product can be transmitted using email.

*   **The rise in self-employment** is perhaps the most significant change in employment patterns in recent years. Self-employment now accounts for 12% of the UK workforce. For many years, the term self-employment typically covered the tradesman type of job. This included those tasks such as repair and maintenance work. In addition, many workers in the construction industry were classed as being self-employed – plasterers, plumbers, painters and decorators. Today, self-employment has moved into many other types of jobs, from haulage work (many lorry drivers are sole proprietors) to insurance and sales persons. As these people carry their work around with them, or base their paperwork activities at home, they have little geographical impact. However, their place within the national economy is not unimportant.

Summary

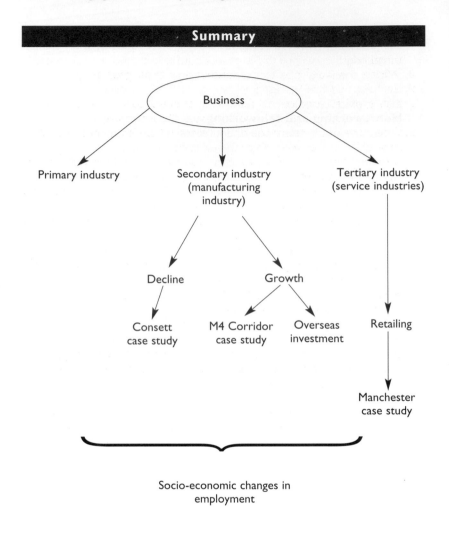

Questions

1.
   a Define the term 'de-industrialisation'.
   b Give five reasons for de-industrialisation in the UK.
2. Choose an area previously dominated by a traditional industry you have studied, and:
   a Outline the traditional industries of that area.
   b Explain why they originated in that area.
   c Discuss the recent changes that have taken place there in terms of industry.

3. Outline the most common features of business and science parks. Suggest reasons why there has been such a rapid growth in these types of industry.

4. What is the likely impact of e-commerce on retail geography?

5.

   a Suggest reasons for the distribution of out-of-town shopping centres.

   b What are the common characteristics of such centres?

6. "The increased personal use of the motor vehicle is the main reason for retail change in the UK". Discuss.

7. 'Working from 9 to 5 was a characteristic of the twentieth century which will not continue into the next century'. Discuss.

8. Visit a local business and/or science park. What industries are located there? What are the main characteristics of the workforce?

9. Visit your local CBD shopping area. Investigate the extent to which there is:

   a clustering of certain types of land-uses within the CBD

   b variation in leisure space (pubs, clubs, theatres etc.) within the CBD

   c socio-economic variation in the use of leisure space

   d variation in terms of age and gender of people within different parts of a city between the day and the evening

10. Visit an out-of-town shopping centre, and:

   a describe its location with respect to transport systems

   b describe the types of shops and other functions located there

   c categorise the advantages and disadvantages of it to people economically, socially and environmentally.

11. Carry out a customer survey of the local garage near you. Where do people travel from to use it? What types of goods do people tend to buy? How often do they shop there? What has been the effect on the local neighbourhood shopping area?

2 Variations in population age structures over time

Age structure: the make-up of a population of a country (or area). It shows the age and sex of a number of sub-groups within the population of that country (area).

Household composition: the degree to which there is a variety of housing types and housing providers within an area. Housing types may be terraced, semi-detached, detached or apartment blocks. Housing providers may be public (council), private, or housing association, with all of these offering the facility to rent or buy.

Segregation: is where certain groups live apart either because they are forced to do so or for economic or social reasons. Segregation of people can be based on race, wealth or age.

Birth rate: a measure of an area's fertility. It is expressed as the number of live births per 1000 people in one year.

Fertility: the average number of children each woman in a population will bear. It is usual to refer to women between the ages of 15 and 50 in such calculations. If fertility is 2.1, then a population will replace itself.

Death rate: the number of deaths in a year per 1000 people.

Infant mortality: the number of deaths of children under the age of one year expressed per thousand live births per year.

Natural change: the change of a population caused by the interrelationship between birth rates and death rates. If birth rates exceed death rates then population increase results. If death rates exceed birth rates then a population will decline.

Life expectancy: the average number of years from birth that a person can expect to live.

Longevity: the increase in life expectancy over a period of time. It is a direct result of improved medical provision and increased levels of economic development. People are living longer and this is creating an increasingly aged population.

Migration: refers to any permanent change of residence by a person. Emigration is the movement of people away from an area to live in another. Immigration is the movement of people into an area.

Annual population change: the cumulative change that results in a population after both natural change and migration have been taken into account.

Population structure: refers to the make-up of a population of an area, usually in the form of age and sex distributions.

1 Introduction

This chapter examines the demographic and social changes affecting the UK during the last 30 years. The major demographic change concerns the ageing of the population, and the implications of this for the future are also reviewed. Other social issues such as housing provision, and the implications of segregation based on wealth, age and ethnicity and on education, health care and housing are also examined.

The population structure of an area changes over time as demographic factors vary. These factors can be listed as:

- birth rates and fertility rates
- death rates, including infant mortality rates
- life expectancy and longevity
- rates of migration in and out of the area.

The most effective way in which these demographic factors can be illustrated is by means of a population pyramid.

2 Population structure

The population pyramid for the UK for the year 2001 shows a relatively straight pyramidal shape, with some slight bulges and indentations in it (Figure 7). The explanation for these slight variations is due to the circumstances that existed at the time when the varying age groups were born, and to factors that have occurred since then.

The slight bulge of people in their 30s demonstrates a period of slightly higher birth rates during the 1960s than in the 1970s. There may be two reasons for this increase in birth rates at this time. Firstly, the 1960s were a period of rising national prosperity and of increases in personal incomes, referred to as the 'Swinging Sixties', a period of the lessening of sexual taboos and of increased female emancipation. Secondly, this was also the time when people who themselves had been born at a time of 'baby boom' after the Second World War were entering their fertile years. As there were more people who were fertile, there would be more babies produced as a result. These people are now in their 50s, and also feature as a slight bulge on the pyramid. These examples demonstrate that population growth is cyclical, and to some extent these changes can be predicted, so long as social norms are retained.

Two further points illustrate this changing nature of population structure. There is a relatively large number of people over the age of 80 in the pyramid. The reasons for this are again complicated. Initially, people born in the period 1910 to 1920 were often part of large families. It was traditional as well as functional to have a large family. Many younger children were expected to die due to endemic diseases, and a large family would act both as a source of income and

Figure 7 The population structure of the UK (2001)

as a form of security in old age. As the century progressed however, fewer and fewer children died (despite the devastating impact of the First World War). Death rates fell massively in the twentieth century as improvements in medical care and the development of new drugs and treatments took place. Thus the people who were born in the early part of the century are now living longer, their longevity is increasing, and particularly so the females.

The second point concerns the younger part of the pyramid. As stated earlier a relative increase in birth rate took place in the 1960s. These people would have become fertile in the 1980s and 1990s, and so a cyclical increase in birth rates would have been expected to take place. This has not happened to the extent predicted. Young adults are now less willing to have children. Various factors have been stated to account for this – a variety of available family planning mechanisms (the contraceptive pill, abortion, sterilisation), the increased desire for material possessions (houses, cars, holidays), and the further emancipation of women enabling them to develop their own careers. With hindsight, it is now possible perhaps to add an additional factor – the economic recession of the late 1980s and early 1990s which left

Population characteristic	Early 1900s	Late 1990s
Population	38 million in 1901	59 million (estimated)
Birth rate	26 per thousand	12.2 per thousand
Infant mortality rate	143 per thousand	5.6 per thousand
Proportion of population 50 and over	17%	32%
Migration rate	800,000 more people migrated out of the UK than into it	60,000 more people migrated into the UK than out of it.

Figure 8 Twentieth-century population changes in the UK

many young adults financially insecure, and forced many women to either go out to work, or to continue to work, as the main 'bread-winner' as male employment in both mining and manufacturing industries fell.

The net result is that the UK now has an ageing population. The proportion of the population aged 50 and over has increased significantly since the start of the century. There has also been a rise in the 'very elderly' – people aged 80 and over. Population projections suggest that these will form over 5% of the population by 2021, when there will be over 3 million of them. At the same time the number of people aged under 16 has been progressively falling. It is anticipated that at some point between 2011 and 2021 the numbers of people 65 and over will exceed those under 16 for the first time.

Figure 8 illustrates some of the major changes in the population of the UK since the early part of this century.

a) The ageing population of the UK

This aspect of the population structure of a country is one which will continue to have major economic and social impacts. In the UK as well as in other MEDCs, welfare provision for the very young, the sick, the disabled, the unemployed and the elderly is a widely accepted government responsibility. However, the costs of such welfare provision are increasing, largely due to the rising numbers of elderly people (Figure 9). Nearly half of all of the benefits paid out by the UK government are for the elderly. For example, it is estimated that over 40% of the budget of the National Health Service is spent on care for the over 65s.

Predictions of the future numbers of elderly people in the UK are alarming, particularly when the economic costs of pensions and

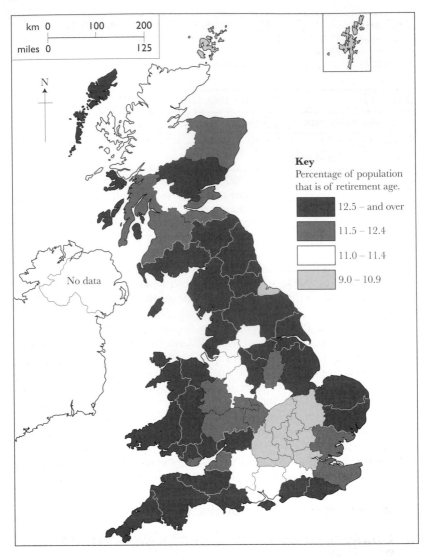

Figure 9 Percentage of retired people in the UK (1996)

health care provision are considered. This is doubly alarming when the fall in the relative numbers of working age people is also considered. The costs of state pensions and other forms of welfare have to be borne by the taxation of people in work. The state pension, introduced in the 1940s, still operates as a 'pay as you work' scheme. The National Insurance and income tax contributions collected from today's workforce goes to today's pensioners through the agency of the government. Many people believe there to be an accumulated fund, and that one pays into that fund for the future – this is not the case. In addition, taxes pay for other social provisions – education and defence for example.

Various UK governments have encouraged the use of private pension schemes, but these have not yet had sufficient time to become widespread, or to become economically strong enough to replace the state pension for many elderly people. The pay out of these policies depends on the profits made by the investment companies, which in turn depend upon the economic strength of the nation as a whole, in other words today's workforce.

The UK government therefore faces a dilemma, known as the 'pensions time bomb'. The pensions of the future will have to be paid for by the people working at that time. But the level of pension payout has already been set. Benefit levels were set at a time when both life expectancy and the amount of elderly people were lower than today. The amount of benefit has steadily increased with inflation, indeed some people have said that they should have risen with the levels of average earnings. The pensioners of today and of tomorrow are understandably unlikely to accept pension payments of a lower economic value than those they were paying for when they were working.

Other factors also come into play. As the number of pensioners grows, they become a more powerful political lobby. Any government would be unwise to ignore or alienate them. Also, more and more people want to retire 'early', and thus potentially exacerbate the situation. Medical research is unlikely to stop, more and more ways of treating disease, cancers and other conditions are being discovered and developed.

Some plans are being made. The retirement age for all people is being raised to 65 (formerly women could retire at 60), and there are proposals to increase it further to 70. Another plan is to make it compulsory for workers to pay into a private pension scheme. A proposal to 'means test' the basic state pension to a greater or lesser extent is also being considered, but this in particular is likely to encounter strong resistance.

3 Changes in household composition in the last 30 years

The character, distribution and availability of housing stock are important elements in urban areas within the UK. There are two main providers – the private sector and the public sector, and individuals can now rent or buy within either of these sectors.

It has always been government policy since the 1940s that improvement should take place in the quality of housing for all groups in society. Up until the late 1970s there were two main thrusts to this policy. Firstly, the private sector was encouraged to provide dwellings for ownership by individuals or families. Private sector rented accommodation was therefore progressively squeezed out. For example, between 1950 and 1980, private house ownership increased from 30% to 56%, and private rented housing decreased from 52% to 12% of all housing tenures. Secondly, the public sector was encouraged to provide rented housing, mainly through the form of local authority council housing subsidised by central government. This resulted in the construction of large council estates on the outskirts of urban areas, together with the building of many council owned high-rise flats in inner city areas. Surprisingly, the proportion of council housing tenure did not increase that greatly between 1950 and 1980 (from 18% to 32%). This can be accounted for by the fact that much of the existing council accommodation was demolished to make way for the new estates and flats.

Following the 1979 General Election and the victory by Margaret Thatcher's Conservative Party, a number of major changes in housing policy came into operation. There were four major changes:

- The Right to Buy legislation of 1980 which gave council tenants the opportunity to buy their homes at discounted prices.
- A reduction in funding for local authority housing by central government.
- Restrictions were placed on local authorities to use the money raised from council house sales to build new homes or renovate existing housing stock.
- The creation of Housing Associations which were private bodies in receipt of government financial support for the building or renovation of dwellings for rent.

These four policies caused an increase of more than 50% in annual building rates by private developers, while completions by the public sector fell by 60%. These changes were not evenly distributed across the country. Demand for private housing rocketed in the economically prosperous areas of the South East. Here, the price of houses rose more rapidly than inflation, fuelled partly by rising land costs. In 1987, for example, the price of the land constituted 53% of the value of the dwelling price, whereas in Yorkshire and Humberside it was only 12%. Consequently, the differential in housing prices widened greatly between the regions. The concept of the North/South divide was enhanced, with the popular view that there were significant problems for the provision of housing in the South East. The construction of new private properties increased greatly in the Greater London and South East areas, and in parts of East Anglia and the East Midlands. Planning permission for such developments was easy to obtain, with little consideration of environmental factors.

At a local level this developed into the idea of the 'haves' and the 'have nots'. The 'haves' were those who could afford to buy into private ownership (often at the cost of great personal financial hardship). The 'have nots' were the poor and deprived whose only housing opportunities lay with either the shrinking housing stock of local authority rental housing, or the new private landlords of the Housing Associations.

a) Changes in the supply of council housing

There are two ways in which a person can obtain a council house. One is through the 'new-build' supply (houses which are newly built by the local authority) and the other is through 're-let' supply (from people who vacate existing properties). During the 1980s the government steadily reduced the amount of money that an authority could use to build new houses. In 1981, a local authority could use 50% of the funds raised by council house sales to build new homes, by 1986 it was 20%. Also by 1986 a further 650,000 council houses had been sold to their occupants, effectively removing them from the stock available. Initially this did not cause too great a problem as many people who lived in council housing were seeking to buy a house from the private sector. Also, with an increasingly elderly population on the former council estates, deaths of tenants and movements into sheltered accommodation were creating sufficient vacancies for new tenants.

However, with the onset of the economic recession in the late 1980s demand for the falling numbers of council housing stock increased greatly. For example, applications for housing from homeless people in English local authorities increased from 220,000 in 1986 to 320,000 in 1996. This new demand for council housing was not evenly spread; London was the area most severely affected.

The role of council housing then came under closer scrutiny. New factors were now coming into play – the rise in the number of divorces, the increase in the number of elderly living alone and the discharge of those with special needs from institutional care. As council house supply dwindled, local authorities increasingly concentrated on those whom they have a statutory duty to house, and those in the most obvious housing need. Council housing has become more and more 'welfare tenure'.

All local authorities have more prospective tenants than vacant properties. Consequently, there are 'waiting lists'. Most waiting list schemes involve the awarding of points to establish priority based on the urgency of the need for housing. Points schemes work by taking into account a number of factors, giving them a certain weight, and adding them together to decide who should be housed first. However, schemes vary in terms of which factors should be considered, and in the relative importance attached to each factor. Examples of these factors include whether or not children are involved; whether the existing dwelling is damp, or has no bathroom; whether a family are currently living with in-laws in an overcrowded house; or how long your name has been on the list. In the decision making process, therefore, it would seem that the attitudes of local councillors and/or officials towards housing needs are more important than consistency and fairness.

b) The boom in private housing construction

As stated in Chapter 1 there has been a significant increase in the numbers of high-tech industries, (both manufacturing and service) in the south east of England, and in particular along the M4 corridor. This rise in employment in such industries has created a demand for private owner occupied housing in counties such as Berkshire. Furthermore, the type of person moving into the area attracted by such employment tends to be more demanding of high quality housing. Consequently, house builders have come under increasing pressure to build for the expensive 'trade-up' market. Many of these have been built on very large sites as developers have been successful in pushing for land release in large blocks and have used central government to override local conservationist councils. During the 1980s, Berkshire County Council came under pressure to release land for up to 8000 homes.

Three issues have arisen from this expansion of owner occupied housing. Firstly, house prices within the area increased at rates faster (over 15%) than the rest of the South East. These high prices probably reflect the high salaries paid to the employees, rather than any absolute shortage of housing stock. Secondly, these high prices make it difficult for people moving into the area and the less affluent living locally to be able to afford adequate housing. Thirdly, the drive for owner occupancy within the area led to an increase in sales of council housing, further reducing the amount of houses in that sector.

The recent growth of private housing has tended to increase rather than decrease social tensions. Those who have campaigned that the construction of new housing areas should be stopped on environmental grounds have become more vociferous. Their objective is to preserve the rural nature of the landscape as much as possible. On the other hand, industrialists point to the need to provide adequate and appropriate housing for the workforce moving into the area. Development control, in the form of green belt land, is increasingly being applied, but this tends to just move the problem to those areas where opposition is less well organised, and away from areas of highest demand. For example, Slough has some of the county's most acute housing problems, and has Berkshire's largest local authority house building programme, yet its growth is restricted by the green belt.

c) Peripheral housing estates

During the 1950s, 1960s and 1970s many local authorities built estates on the edges of their urban areas. These were mainly to house overspill population, and those needing to be rehoused due to slum clearance. The estates consisted of houses of typical council design – uniform red brick with or without cement rendering, semi-detached with gardens, metal framed windows, limited garaging, and the distinctive sequenced colours of their front doors. Within these estates there were also system-built tower blocks and maisonettes made of prefabricated materials. The relative construction costs of these types of housing were low, and were therefore favoured by local authorities in order to meet housing demand cheaply. Planning controls were very limited, and construction was done in excessive haste. Indeed, with time considerable evidence of corruption by local authority leaders in the issuing of lucrative contracts for both the design and construction of these properties has emerged.

It all seemed such a good idea at the time to build these estates. Greenfield sites were used to build large estates and to provide decent homes for the poorer elements of society, as well as provide areas of open space and public amenities. Communities the size of small towns were constructed on the outskirts of cities but without the necessary facilities and links to the city centre or places of work.

During the 1980s and 1990s the physical fabric of these estates deteriorated markedly, and the environmental quality of the streets and open spaces became poor. Maintenance costs for these estates

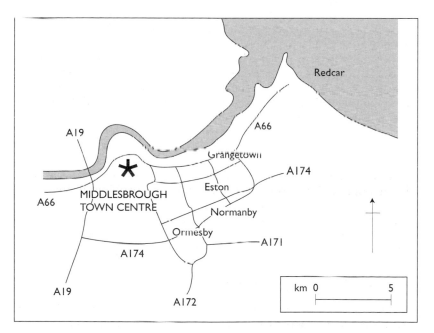

Figure 10 Housing estates in East Middlesbrough

escalated to the point that in many cases demolition was the most favoured and most practical option. The houses and flats have not proved popular under the Right to Buy legislation, and so many have remained in rental tenure. One result of this has been that such estates contain above average proportions of the more vulnerable groups in society – low income households, the unemployed, the poor elderly. They are becoming the centre of a whole range of social and economic problems.

One such area is to the east of Middlesbrough (Figure 10). East Middlesbrough has eleven estates (in Eston, Normanby and Ormesby) within an area of 2 square miles containing over 10,000 homes, only 20% of which are privately owned. The housing is pre-dominantly two storey terraced semi-detached with gardens. Some installation of central heating has taken place together with double glazing. Most of the three and four storey maisonettes have been removed, but the high rise flats remain. These have had some improvement but there are still problems of damp and security.

The problems of the area are more to do with the people than the property. The biggest problem is unemployment, male unemploy-ment is 30–40%. The decline of the traditional industries of ship-building, chemicals and engineering has been the major cause of this. Unemployment means low income, and when added to the retired people living in the area, it is not surprising to find that 70% of the council tenants are in receipt of housing benefit. Social problems of marriage breakdown, low academic attainment, drug abuse and petty crime are endemic. An additional problem is that of isolation – many of the estates are 4–5 miles from the city centre, and transport is an unaffordable luxury. Car ownership is low. Appropriate facilities are provided but they are restricted and choice is limited. Each estate tends to look inwards rather than outwards, and this makes aspiration for its people low. Few people who do not live in these estates will have cause to visit them.

d) Housing Associations

Housing Associations were originally set up in the 1970s as an alterna-tive to local authority council housing, to provide rented accommo-dation in a non-profit making capacity. However, as the role of the local authority as a provider of rented housing began to diminish, Housing Associations took on a greater significance during the 1980s and beyond.

Before the 1988 Housing Act, Housing Associations were under-written by the government, their rents were fixed by independent officers and any shortfall between income from rents and costs were subsidised by a grant from central government. Since the 1988 Act, the emphasis has changed. No longer are they intended to be sup-ported fully by national government. They are encouraged to borrow capital from private investors, and in some cases local authorities, and to seek a return on their housing investments. They are now expected to be profitable. Subsidies are still available for some areas, which enables them to charge relatively low rents in those areas; consequently a major role is still to provide rented accommodation for the poor, the elderly, single parents and the handicapped. During the 1990s the share of rented accommodation run by Housing Associations doubled, although their properties are still lower in absolute numbers than local authorities.

Housing Associations are also subject to the Right to Buy legislation along with council owned property. One way in which they have assisted in this is in the purchasing of empty properties, refurbishing these and then selling them on to private buyers. Once again financial assistance has been made available by central government for this purpose.

Another feature of their changing role is the movement into shared ownership. This is where the purchaser pays for a proportion of the value of the house. The Housing Association pays the rest of the price, and then the purchaser pays rent for that proportion of the house. This is a way in which people with limited resources can make a start towards owning their own house. Some Housing Associations also offer furniture rental packages, whereby basic furniture items (beds, wardrobes, cooker, fridge and chairs) are available on a rental basis.

Case study: The Stockbridge Village Trust – an example of a Housing Association scheme

On the eastern edge of Liverpool can be found the Cantril Farm estate, part of Knowsley Metropolitan Borough Council. The estate was built in the 1960s to re-house displaced people from slum clearance schemes in the centre of Liverpool into two storey houses, maisonettes and high rise flats. In many ways the estate was typical of the housing redevelopment of that time. In 1983, the estate was purchased by the Stockbridge Village Trust with loans from banks, building societies and the Knowsley Council itself. The estate comprised 3000 homes which were deteriorating in varying degrees, and there were also signs of movement out by the population to the extent that it was predicted that half the estate would be empty by the mid 1990s.

The Trust was established as a non-profit making association with four main aims:

* to demolish the most unpopular and unsafe buildings
* to refurbish the remaining housing stock
* to develop new private housing for sale and rent

- to redevelop the service provision of the estate, in particular shopping and leisure facilities.

The Trust was supported by national government at the time. An allocation of urban programme funds was made available, and the Merseyside Task Force had been established to coordinate the variety of initiatives in the Merseyside area. By 1985 the pace of change was not as fast as had been hoped for. The costs of refurbishment of each house doubled the original estimate (£6700 rather than £3000), the cost of redeveloping the shopping centre had risen from £2 million to £6 million, and only a small number of private houses for sale had been built and sold.

There were two main difficulties. Rents were the main source of income, but these were subject to the Fair Rents Legislation. Secondly, incomes in the area were low such that few people could afford to buy those houses that they wished to buy under the Right to Buy scheme. The financial position of the Trust gave cause for concern, made worse by the high interest rates prevalent at the time. It was clear that further support from local and national government was necessary, or else the scheme would collapse.

The Department for the Environment and Knowsley Council had to provide an extra £5 million between them. By 1987 most of the housing stock had been refurbished. Over 250 new houses had been built for rent, and a private developer had constructed over 125 houses all of which had been sold. The Trust built a new shopping centre, and Knowsley Council started work on a new leisure centre. The demolition of the high rise flats also began.

During the 1990s the objectives of the Trust were to continue its housing programme. Housing repairs continued as well as a move to broaden the type of tenure. A further 250 new houses were constructed, some for rent and some for shared ownership. Private developers were also encouraged to add further properties to the area. The management role of the Housing Association is one of ensuring close collaboration between the public and private sectors towards the common goal of the provision of good quality housing for all.

As time has progressed, the objectives of the Trust have generally been achieved. The quality of housing in the area has improved, out-migration has been reduced (although not stopped), and home ownership (both individual and shared) has increased. However, the concerns regarding maintenance of the properties remain, as properties continue to decay with time. Personal incomes in the area remain below the national average, and there is still a reluctance by individuals to invest large sums of their own money in home improvements.

e) Where are we going to live in the twenty-first century?

Population projections for the UK suggest that between 1991 and 2021 the population of the country will rise by over 5 million, an increase of just under 10%. At the same time the number of households will increase at a faster rate, rising to nearly 24 million in total. Each new household will require its own housing unit, which means more houses and flats will need to be built.

What is the cause of this large rate in the growth of households? There are three main reasons for this:

- The growth in the number of people in certain parts of the country is the main reason. There will be a migration of people into southern England from other parts of the UK, and this will cause an increase in the demand for housing.
- More and more people are choosing to live on their own for longer periods of time. This may be due to the incidence of later marriages, and higher divorce rates.
- As people live longer, so the proportion of people in the younger age groups falls, and the amount of single elderly people increases.

One possible solution to this issue is to increase the number of people living in existing homes. Across the country there are 1 million empty properties, 90% of which are in the private sector. Government policies are endeavouring to reduce the number of empty homes so that up to 250,000 homes become available.

Another approach that has been suggested is to encourage people to take in lodgers. This would be a cheap option, and would not use up valuable land. However, many of the available properties are sited in unpopular places – perhaps the main reason why they are empty in the first place.

The main debate, however, is whether we should build new houses in rural areas (on greenfield sites) or in urban areas (on brownfield sites). Greenfield land is land which has not been developed before and includes wasteland that no one ever wanted to build on, protected areas such as green belt land, parks, golf courses and playing fields. Brownfield land is land which has previously been developed for industry, offices and former housing areas. Not all brownfield sites are empty, they may still have derelict buildings on them. The government has set a target for 60% of new houses to be on brownfield land, although some environmental organisations would like it to be nearer to 75%. Both of these are unlikely to be achieved as:

- There is a mismatch between where land is available and where it is most needed.
- Much greenfield land has already received planning permission for housing.
- The supply of brownfield land is limited. It is often in undesirable

locations and has high development costs due to the need to clear old buildings and to remove industrial contamination.

The advantages of brownfield sites are well stated. People living in these houses will live close to their place of work, and shopping and leisure facilities. They will be more able to use public transport systems, and therefore less reliant on the private car. Pollution and energy use will be reduced. Existing rural communities and lifestyles would also be protected.

Those who advocate the development of greenfield sites claim that the land is cheaper to develop, and that there is plenty of land available, particularly with large tracts of rural land now being underused as farmland (for example under the European Union set aside policy). In 1991, 10.6% of land in England was classified as being urban, and by 2021 this will rise to only 12% if all development plans are agreed.

One of the most alarming trends in the 1990s has been the increase in the use of urban greenfield land, such as parts of parks and school playing fields. In this decade, 61% of new housing was in urban areas, but 12% of this was on such 'green' areas.

A considerable proportion of new houses will be built in the South East of England. There are three main options as to where this development takes place:

*   by extending existing towns
*   by extending existing villages
*   by building new towns and villages.

If the third option is the answer, then the best locations will be those served by existing routeways and public transport systems. Already, the government is considering the possible location of new towns near Ashford in Kent, Crawley in West Sussex, and Stansted in Essex.

4 The geographical segregation of social groups

The segregation of social groups involves distinct groups of people living almost entirely separately. It produces clusters of people with similar characteristics in separate residential areas within an urban area. Examples of social segregation that has taken place in UK cities relate to personal wealth, age and ethnicity.

The concept of social segregation is not new to cities in MEDCs. In the USA for example, the black ghetto is a common feature of many cities. These are areas where the population is predominantly, if not exclusively, of African American race. Similarly, 'quarters' or 'quartiers' which are associated with particular ethnic or national groups such as Italian and Jewish people exist in many cities. Often these people live and work in the area, and are linked to particular occupations or services.

All of these social groupings so far mentioned refer to ethnicity, nationality and religion. However, there are other ways in which social segregation may occur – through wealth and through age. Many towns and cities in the UK are characterised by poorer and more wealthy people living in distinct residential areas. For many years the simple distinction was one of the poorer people living near the city centres, and the more wealthy living on the outskirts or in the suburbs. This simple pattern has been complicated by the construction of peripheral council housing estates with large concentrations of poorer people. The gentrification or upgrading of the housing stock of some inner city areas also goes against this simple dichotomy.

Segregation may also be by age group, and there are signs of this increasing in many towns and cities in the UK. As the number of elderly and the age to which they live have increased, so the providers of specialised housing have become more interested in them. This housing has often been located in specific parts of a town, either in the form of newly built and designed sheltered accommodation, or in the form of converted former large town houses. Gender is a related factor here. Life expectancy amongst females is significantly greater than that for males, so their needs and wishes have to be considered specifically.

The reasons for segregation of these types are complex, but can be summarised in the following ways:

- Social groups of various types may choose to live in separate areas, or they may be constrained to do so. The reality is often a combination of the two. For example, ethnic minorities dominate certain areas of a town because originally these areas were the areas with the cheapest costs of accommodation, when the original migrants had low wealth and worked in low income jobs. With time the areas developed their own characteristics and support mechanisms which made them more suitable and attractive to new migrants to the town. The people retain their own identity and preserve their customs, traditions and faiths.
- Once created, social divisions tend to be accentuated through lack of contact or interaction with other social groupings. Stereotypical viewpoints develop, of the elderly, or of the poor, and there is no real understanding of one group by the rest of society. Existing differences become prolonged or exacerbated, and fear or suspicion add to the feeling of 'them' and 'us'. The segregation continues and increases as one group feels more safe in its own segregated area. Social tensions often arise, which sometimes manifest themselves in more extreme ways, further adding to the lack of integration. The problems related to ethnic segregation which surfaced in Oldham and Leeds in 2001 illustrate these tensions.
- It is surprising how often a physical barrier may encourage social segregation, for example, a main road or a railway line. Such a feature may separate a council estate from a private housing estate, or a fence may separate a gentrified up-market housing area from its poorer surroundings. Such barriers mark out relative territories and act to reduce interaction even more.

Whatever the main basis of the segregation, there have been significant effects on the provision of housing, education and health care within many towns and cities in the UK.

a) Segregation based on wealth

Many urban areas are characterised by poorer and richer people living in very different neighbourhoods. The general pattern has been one of the poor living in the inner cities, and the rich living in the outer areas. Peripheral council estates with concentrations of poorer people have complicated this pattern. Similarly, the gentrification of some inner areas has inverted the original pattern even more. Now richer people live very near to poorer people in the inner cities, although the amount of interaction between them is still low.

i) The effects on housing

Areas on the edge of many cities are still occupied by the wealthy, for example, Alwoodley in Leeds, and Bramhall, Cheadle Hulme and Alderley Edge in Greater Manchester. This latter area is inhabited by commuters who work in Manchester and further afield, who command high incomes for their work. Houses in the area regularly sell for over £250,000, substantially more than many other areas in the city of Manchester. Car ownership in the area is high at 86%, compared with the national average of 67%.

Many inner city areas are still poor, for example Harehills in Leeds, and Ancoats in central Manchester. Ancoats lies to the north of Piccadilly station and consists mostly of council housing in the form of two-storey houses, maisonettes and high rise flats. The car ownership of the area is well below the national average at 16% indicating the low levels of personal wealth in the area. Unemployment is high and the environmental quality is poor, with much derelict land. Restoration of the area is progressing at pace, but it is still an example which fits the traditional view of a poor inner city area.

Prestigious inner city areas have always been popular with some wealthy groups of society. In London, the areas of Mayfair, Belgravia, Chelsea and Kensington have never lost their status. In recent years these have been added to by other fashionable locations within the city. Notting Hill, Islington and Primrose Hill are becoming increasingly popular with the rich and famous.

As described earlier in the section on East Middlesbrough (page 38), a great deal of council house development has occurred on the edges of cities, for example Seacroft (Leeds), and Newall Green (Manchester). This has led to the spread of poorer people into the periphery of many towns and cities.

To counter this movement, in recent years, gentrification has occurred in many inner-city areas, for example, the riverside area in Leeds, and Castlefields area in Manchester. Pockets of high status housing exist in inner city areas where there is a highly favoured environment, and where redevelopment has made the area desirable to live in again. The London Docklands with its new marinas, luxury converted warehouses and spectacular river views is another well documented example of this phenomenon.

ii) The effects on education

Schools tend to be evenly spread, reflecting population coverage, although higher concentrations of older Victorian schools are still located in many poorer inner city areas. Most of these still operate as primary schools, with the characteristic separate entrances for boys and girls still labelled above doorways. It is rare to find secondary schools dating back to this era. Most secondary schools in such areas consist of the same modern and cheaper building materials that make up the new housing areas around them.

Out-of-town council estates usually have purpose-built comprehensives within them. As with similar schools in the inner city, these tend to be built to the same design specification. They consist of rectangular building blocks, up to three storeys in height, with a spread of flat-roofed single storey buildings around them. In recent years, a great deal of maintenance work has had to be undertaken on these school buildings, particularly in terms of flat roof drainage and asbestos removal.

Each major new housing development tends to have its own primary school. However, this is not the case when new, often small, private housing areas are being developed in the vicinity of existing housing areas. Such developments can place the primary schools in the area under pressure in terms of both places and class sizes. In some cases, it is the good reputation of the school that has encouraged the building of the housing development, as people with high aspirations for their younger children strive to gain access to a 'good school'. There are even some suggestions that the perceived quality of the secondary school (which children will enter some years in the future) can influence housing decisions. School 'catchment area' decision-making is becoming more influential with time. This is a good example of the close interdependence between private sector development (housing) and public sector provision (education), for which it is difficult to have overall strategic planning.

The quality of educational facilities therefore varies within a town, with older schools usually found in poorer areas. These are often vandalised and in a poor physical state with crumbling buildings. Out-of-town comprehensives based in low income council estates are also facing similar problems. It has been recognised that there is a great danger that some of these are becoming educational backwaters with low educational attainment, low rates of attendance and high levels of truancy.

In those parts of urban areas with higher personal incomes, there tends to be less of this type of problem. As stated above, the major problem appears to be one of demand for places both at primary and secondary school level. Such demand may be one of the factors leading to higher house prices in these areas. There is also a greater incidence of private schools being established in these areas, as well as those schools which have opted out of local authority control (formerly known as Grant Maintained schools). There is currently a range of initiatives that schools can subscribe to, such as Technology College and Language College status, which are more likely to be found in the more affluent parts of an urban area than the less affluent.

iii) The effects on health care
There are two types of medical provision that can be examined, the smaller scale doctor's surgery, or medical centre, and the large scale hospital.

There is often a greater demand for medical centre facilities in poorer areas, possibly due to there being proportionately more young children and elderly people. Also population densities are lower in wealthy areas, so proportionately fewer such surgeries are located there. These facilities in wealthy areas are less likely to be purpose-built, there is more conversion of private houses. On the other hand, less affluent areas are more likely to have purpose-built single storey facilities, in the form of health centres. In many cases these are geographically linked to either a small shopping centre, or a residential nursing home for the elderly or both. Some larger medical centres of this type may indeed offer out-patient facilities from the local hospital, or even carry out surgical operations of a less critical nature.

Hospital location is more variable, but there is still a concentration of National Health Service (NHS) hospitals in the older, more central parts of a town or city. Consequently, they are accessible to the poorer (public transport access), and the more wealthy alike (car access). Modern hospital construction tends to take place on the edge of a town. Here the same benefits that apply to an out-of-town shopping complex apply. Road transport is easier, and there is space for expansion and for car parking. However, the analogy with shopping also applies in terms of problems caused. Those with lower incomes, the unemployed and elderly, have difficulties gaining access, largely through the limited car ownership of these groups. Ambulance provision is not normally affected by these developments as it is common to find that ambulance depots are spread evenly within an urban area.

Private hospitals have a variable locational pattern. Some tend to be located in pleasant wealthy suburbs, others are located on major routeways out of town, and some are very close to the NHS provision due to the need to share expertise and personnel. There are some private facilities that are located well away from the urban area altogether. There is also a mixture of both purpose built provision in some areas and the conversion and extension of existing property in others.

Finally, there have been some changes in recent years in provision for the mentally ill. In the 1970s and before, the solution was the 'lunatic asylum', a hospital for the mentally ill frequently located on the edge of a town, or at some distance from it. These were of Victorian red brick construction, with extensive gardens or estates around them. Very few people had cause to visit them. The mentally ill were thus segregated from the rest of society. In recent years the management of the mentally ill has changed to one of 'Care in the Community'. Here the idea is one of integration and treatment within the community; that is, within cities themselves. Unfortunately, this has not been as successful as intended. The number of homeless people, many of whom were or would have been placed in the former asylums, has increased greatly. These and other socially and economically unfortunate people are now very much concentrated in the inner city areas, either as homeless or living in hostels.

b) Segregation based on age

As the number of elderly and the age to which they live increases, so some degree of segregation has taken place, particularly in terms of housing. The decision facing many elderly people is whether or not they want to leave the family home when they are left on their own or have difficulty caring for themselves. The move to another area where there are larger numbers of people of roughly similar ages is likely to be traumatic, and consideration of whether this is the best for the individual and for society has to be borne in mind.

Old people living in council houses on their own have found that very often they do not have a choice of whether to leave or stay. Housing Departments have moved them out into sheltered accommodation or nursing homes because they require the house for a family.

Segregation based on age has manifested itself in a number of ways in towns in the UK:

- On council estates it is common to see clusters of purpose-built bunga-lows occupying one small part of the estate. This has developed in some areas into the provision of maisonnettes with security access. This has followed the belief that elderly people are best living in the community for as long as they are fit and healthy to do so. These people have often lived in the area for a long time. They have friends and relatives there and they are integrated into social functions such as those linked with a church or clubs.
- A more recent provision has been sheltered accommodation – a flat or unit within a larger complex with some shared facilities, overseen by a warden or manager. In some cases purpose-built blocks of flats, some for single people and some for married couples have been constructed. This concept has developed into there being a mobile warden who may

cover a number of complexes. The location of these facilities is only just beginning to establish a pattern in some urban areas.

- Nursing homes have been increasing as the number of elderly who have difficulty looking after themselves increases. Initially, both local authorities and private developers provided such housing, but local authorities have been cutting back in their provision in recent years. In many urban areas, concentrations of nursing homes are becoming clear. They are often in both inner and outer suburbs, in areas where large Georgian and Victorian houses can either be converted and/or extended for this purpose. Close links with medical provision are also a factor, and it has been suggested that some of the most financially successful nursing homes are located on a main road within a town so as to facilitate the arrival of ambulances

c) Segregation based on ethnicity

Ethnic segregation is the clustering together of people with similar ethnic or cultural characteristics into separate residential areas in an urban area. There are numerous examples of this in many urban areas within the UK. The Indian population is the largest ethnic minority in the country, forming 27% of the total ethnic minority population (Figure 11). The next largest is the Pakistani ethnic minority (17%), closely followed by the Black-Caribbean (15%). Smaller, but still significant, ethnic minorities of Bangladeshi (Figure 12), Black-African and Chinese also exist in the country.

Ethnic minorities are concentrated in major urban areas in the UK, particularly London and the South East, the West and East Midlands, Manchester and West Yorkshire. Over 50% of ethnic minorities live in the South East, which has only 30% of the white population. A significant proportion of ethnic minorities are now born in the UK, descended from people who arrived from the former Commonwealth countries in the 1960s and 1970s. There are large concentrations of Indians in the East and West Midlands (Leicester, Wolverhampton and Sandwell for example), and Lancashire (Blackburn for example). The Pakistani minority is concentrated in parts of Bradford, Leeds and Birmingham, and there are large Bangladeshi communities in Luton, Oldham and Birmingham.

The 1991 Census brought to light some geographical variations within urban areas between some ethnic minorities. Bangladeshi and Black-Caribbean groups are concentrated in high density inner city areas characterised by low levels of owner occupancy and high levels of unemployment. In contrast, people of Chinese origin are distributed across a wide range of areas – from deprived inner-city areas to more affluent suburbs. There is some research that suggests that ethnic segregation is more geographically pronounced in northern areas than in London. Although London has a very high proportion of ethnic minorities, the sheer diversity of the ethnic population and

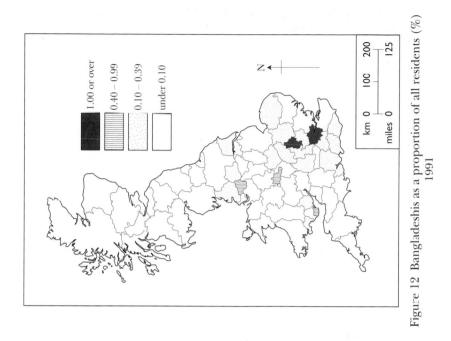

Figure 12 Bangladeshis as a proportion of all residents (%) 1991

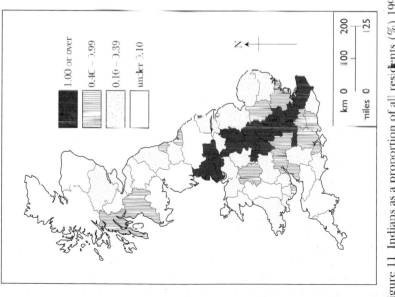

Figure 11 Indians as a proportion of all residents (%) 1991

the lack of insularity that this has created prevents extreme forms of segregation from developing.

The ethnic minority population is generally younger than the white population of the UK. In the mid 1990s, there were particularly large concentrations in the young adult (25 to 44) category, with fewer in the older age groups (particularly over 75). At this time the median age for all the ethnic minorities was 25 years, compared with 37 years for the white population.

Unemployment amongst the ethnic population has a complex pattern. The group with the highest rates of economic inactivity is the Bangladeshi population. Here, over 50% of the population over 16 years is economically inactive. However, this is partly a consequence of the low employment rate of working age Bangladeshi women, only one in five of women aged between 16 and 59 are in employment, which is itself a consequence of Islamic cultural traditions. On the other hand, male unemployment in the Chinese community is below that of the white population.

i) The effects on housing

In the initial phases of immigration, multiple occupancy in rented accommodation in inner city areas (terraced houses) was widespread. Ethnic minorities have been much less successful in securing conventional mortgage loans and this has forced them to take less conventional and more expensive forms of financing which then limits the price of housing they are able to afford. The prospect of an expensive mortgage on a sub-standard property in a deprived area contributed to the low rate of owner occupancy amongst the ethnic minority population.

Ethnic minorities have also been discriminated against in terms of access to local authority housing and as a result are disproportionately represented. This has led, in a number of urban areas, to the development of internal networks of housing provision, where landlords of one ethnic group provide housing for that ethnic group – a process known as the 'racialisation of residential space.'

Later, owner occupancy has arisen with movements of some more wealthy individuals out into suburban areas. Also, many people run a small business, with housing being part of the same building.

ii) The effects on education

Concentrations of minorities in inner city areas have led to some schools being dominated by one ethnic group, with consequent effects on education requirements, for example, special English lessons for children and their parents (mothers in particular), and bilingual reading schemes. In the more traditional parts of some cities, special religious provision is deemed necessary by the minority groups. This has developed into a call for separate schooling in some areas, but only in a minority of cases.

The variation in the educational attainment of the different ethnic minorities is still being examined. There is some evidence to suggest that children from Black-Caribbean and Bangladeshi backgrounds are underperforming compared with not only the white population but also other ethnic groups. Conversely, the performance of children from Indian, Pakistani and Chinese backgrounds appears to be better than that of the white population. Indeed, it is said that it is the white working class male that is the lowest achiever at the moment in schools.

iii) The effects on health care

In the early phases of immigration there were problems associated with the lack of resistance to childhood diseases by immigrant children, and fears over immunisation. Literature in ethnic minority languages aimed at educating immigrant parents had to be produced. However, as literacy and educational standards have improved, particularly amongst second and subsequent generation immigrants, there have been fewer concerns. As many ethnic minority groups continue to live in inner city areas (which still tend to be more run down), there remains a higher concentration of communicable and transmittable disease in such areas. But this is more a reflection of the living standards of the areas rather than of the people who live in them.

Summary

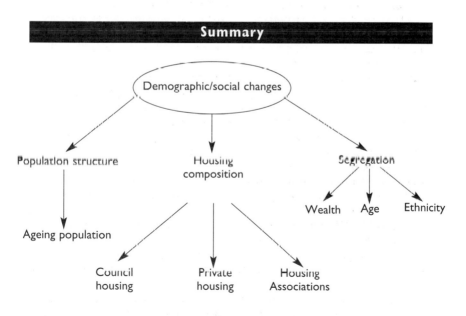

Questions

1. Distinguish between the terms 'life expectancy' and 'longevity'.
2.
   a Why have death rates fallen in the UK in the last 50 years?
   b Why have birth rates fallen in the UK in the last 50 years?
3.
   a What are the likely changes to the population structure of the UK over the next 30 years?
   b What will be the impact of these changes on welfare provision within the country?
4. Describe the major changes in housing tenure that have taken place in the UK since 1980. Suggest reasons for these changes.
5. 'Council housing is for the poor; private housing is for the rich.' With reference to examples you have studied, discuss the validity of this statement.
6. Discuss the role played by Housing Associations in the provision of low cost housing in the UK.
7. 'The South East of England is the area where most new housing is needed in this country. Planners and builders should be allowed to meet this demand.' Discuss this statement.
8. With reference to examples, state what is meant by the term 'social segregation'.
9. Why does social segregation develop in the urban areas of the UK?
10. Discuss the effects of segregation based on wealth on the social provision of housing, education and health care.
11. With reference to an urban area you have studied, describe the effects of segregation based on age.
12. 'Segregation based on ethnicity within urban areas in the UK is decreasing in scale.' Discuss the extent to which you agree with this statement.
13. Examine Figure 13 which shows ethnic segregation in Bradford.
    a Compare the distributions of the different ethnic groups shown.
    b Suggest reasons for patterns of ethnic segregation in Bradford.
    c Discuss the issues that have arisen in one or more cities where segregation based on ethnicity has taken place.
14. Obtain census data for the area where you live. The data can be processed either in terms of ward scale or enumeration district scale. You should be able to access data that gives a range of demographic, social and economic information, such as sex, age groups, % unemployed, % of households with no car, housing tenure, % of people in non-white ethnic groups (as well as each ethnic group), and many others.
    a Analyse the main aspects of the population of the ward, and compare them with other wards in the same town.
    b Construct population pyramids, or choropleth maps of a variety of aspects, or carry out statistical analyses of the data.
15. Visit your Local Authority Housing Department, and/or Planning Department. Ask for details of the current patterns of housing tenure

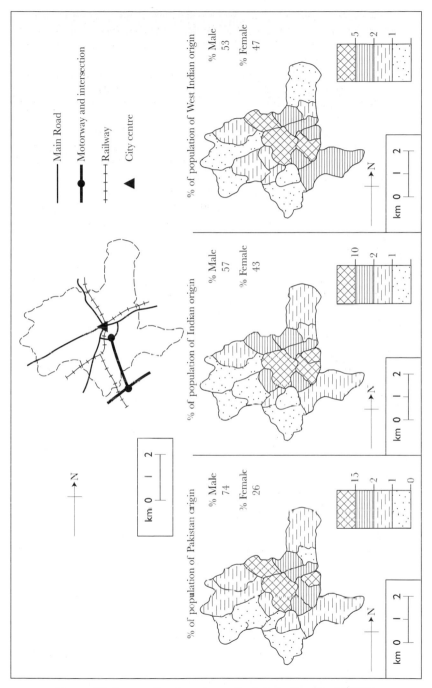

Figure 13 Segregation based on ethnicity in Bradford (2001)

within your area, and details of the Structure Plan for future housing needs. Interview a representative from the Housing Department to find out what problems affect council estates in your area. How does their 'waiting list' scheme operate?

16. Visit the offices of a major private housing developer in your area. Where are they currently building houses? What problems did they face in obtaining planning permission for those houses? Where do they intend to build in the future?

17. Visit the offices of a local Housing Association. Where do they currently manage houses in your area? How has their role changed over the last 20 years, and have there been any changes in the nature of the people renting properties from them?

18. Visit the local Planning Department in your town. Ask for a map showing the extent of the green belt around your town. Are there any plans to modify this map, either in terms of reducing or enlarging the area of green belt land?

19. Carry out an investigation to assess the extent of social segregation by age in your town. Map the locations of purpose built bungalows, sheltered accommodation and nursing homes within the town. What factors may account for these patterns?

20. Carry out an investigation to assess the pattern of health care provision within your town. Locate all the General Practitioner (GP) surgeries in the town, and map them. Identify the numbers of people on the medical lists of each GP, and try to match provision to need. Do other factors such as age or income of the surrounding people appear to influence provision? To what extent is there a relationship between the location of GP surgeries and the location of pharmacies (chemists)?

3 Inner cities

KEY WORDS

Inner city: those areas of a town or city lying immediately outside the Central Business District, but before the suburbs. The housing areas tend to be old (mainly nineteenth century) and rundown, and industrial property is often declining or derelict. Other aspects of poverty can frequently be seen as well as signs of social malaise.

Regeneration: the investment of capital and ideas into an area to revitalise and renew its economic, social and environmental condition.

1 Introduction

This chapter examines the causes of decline in inner city areas within the UK within the last 30 years. Decline has been caused by a range of economic, social and environmental factors. The subsequent attempts to regenerate these areas, by a variety of governments, are then reviewed, with use being made of a range of case studies.

2 The causes of inner city decline

Over 4 million people live in the inner cities of the UK. These areas are typified by economic decline, personal poverty, social problems and environmental decay. They are also areas where political strength has waned, but where political discontent is often more visible.

a) Economic decline

Since the 1950s there has been a widespread movement of employment away from the large conurbations to smaller urban areas and to rural areas. This fall in employment has largely taken place in the traditional manufacturing industries formerly based on coal, steam power and railways. These industries had their location in today's inner city areas. Between 1960 and 1981, over 1.6 million manufacturing jobs were lost in the major urban areas of the country, which accounted for three-quarters of the national job losses of that time (Figure 14).

This decline in manufacturing was accompanied by a growth in employment in service industries. This growth, however, did not compensate for the massive job losses in manufacturing. In addition, service industries did not require the same skills required by manufacturing industry. Towards the end of the 1980s and the early

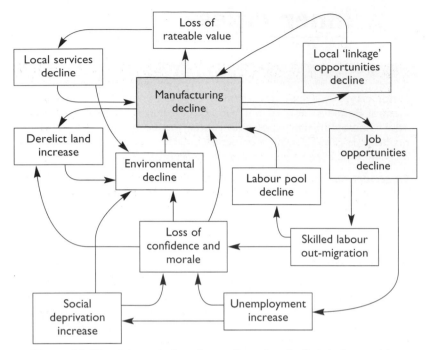

Figure 14 The vicious circles of manufacturing decline in inner cities

1990s the service industries in the inner cities also faced job losses. Employment in services fell in inner city areas by 7% compared with a national increase in such jobs of 11%.

This de-industrialisation in the inner cities was accompanied by the expansion of both the manufacturing and service sector forms of employment in rural areas and small towns. This shift is explained more fully in Chapter 1, but can be summarised as follows. It is partly explained by the changing levels of technology and space require-ments of manufacturing industry which resulted in a shortage of suit-able land and premises in the inner cities. This had the effect of diverting investment and employment growth from urban to rural locations. Another key cause was global economic change which led to declining profits and increased competition for British industry. To remain competitive companies were forced to restructure their pro-duction methods and labour requirements. This restructuring involved the acquisition of other companies, the introduction of new technology, and the geographical movement of investment to new locations in the UK and overseas. The employment losses that were caused were skewed towards the inner cities because they contained many of the types of workplaces most likely to be closed down. These were the older plants with the oldest production techniques, lowest productivity and most highly unionised workforces.

Unemployment thus became a major problem for the inner city area of the former industrial regions of Liverpool, Sheffield, Glasgow, Newcastle upon Tyne, and Birmingham. The period of unemployment for individuals grew longer, and were particularly high amongst school leavers, the poorly qualified, the poorly skilled and ethnic minorities. In 1994, the inner cities of the UK had an unemployment rate 50% higher than the rest of the country.

b) Population loss and social decline

Between 1951 and 1981, the UK's largest conurbations lost 35% of their population and migration was the key cause of these changes. For example, the out-migration of population from inner areas of Liverpool and Manchester led to a population decline of over 25% in the 1970s. Many of these people migrated away from inner city areas in search of better employment opportunities. In the 1960s and 1970s the out-movement of people led to the growth of small towns around the large conurbations. In the 1980s a significant proportion of the out-migration from cities involved people moving to rural areas, a process known as counter-urbanisation. The key causes of population decline in the inner cities therefore are changing residential preferences, job growth and improvements in accessibility in suburban and rural areas, as well as the poor image of the inner city.

The people who have left the inner city areas have tended to be the younger, the more affluent and the more skilled. This has meant that those left behind are the less-skilled and the poor. Economic decline of these areas therefore led to social decline.

c) The poor physical environment

The physical environment of the inner cities is usually poor with low quality housing, empty and derelict properties, vacant factories, and unsightly overgrown waste land. The physical deterioration of inner city environments is characterised by high levels of vandalism, dereliction, graffiti and flyposting. These areas also have low levels of public environmental amenities such as parks, open spaces and play areas. A more recent feature is the construction of urban motorways, with their flyovers, underpasses and networks of pedestrian walkways which contribute further to the bleak concrete-based landscape.

Some of this dereliction is due to the continued existence of remnants of nineteenth century terraced housing, which is now often of poor quality. However, slum clearance schemes of the 1960s and 1970s created equally unsightly estates of poorly constructed houses and high rise flats. Many of these have been demolished, but some still remain as unpopular and difficult living environments.

d) Political problems

There has been increasing concern that the problems of the inner city residents have been marginalised politically. At one scale there have been political clashes between local inner city government and central government. At another, inner cities have the lowest turnout rates in elections in the UK, reflecting the degree to which the people feel rejected. Left wing political groups have used the inner cities to press home their attacks on more conservative elements in politics. Political tension has been heightened by the limited impacts of urban regeneration policies which have led to a large amount of physical redevelopment whilst the long standing levels of social and economic deprivation remain largely unchanged.

3 Urban regeneration policies

Since the end of the 1970s there has been a large number of urban regeneration policies brought about by national government. Local governments have initiated their own programmes broadly in line with national policies, but retaining some degree of autonomy. The early 1990s mark a threshold by which urban regeneration schemes can be described. Either side of this period saw a difference in approach to the issue of inner city redevelopment.

a) Urban regeneration schemes 1967–79

During this time, the UK was governed by both Labour and Conservative administrations. Attention was focussed by both types of government on the inner city zones where decentralisation, de-industrialisation and decline had set in. These areas were also those of inward migration by the ethnic minorities – places such as Brixton in London, Chapeltown in Leeds, and Moss Side in Manchester.

In 1968, the **Urban Aid Programme** was established by which government grants for a huge range of small-scale projects such as housing renovation, community advice centres, nursery schools and other community development schemes were made available. In 1969, **General Improvement Areas (GIAs)** were established, and in 1974 **Housing Action Areas** were created. The approach of GIAs was to boost areas of fundamentally sound housing, through the use of improvement grants, together with the introduction of a series of measures that sought to improve the street environment such as pedestrianisation, landscaping, and the provision of play space and off-street parking. Housing Actions Areas targeted the very worst housing conditions which were also the areas of multiple deprivation and social stress. In 1967, **Education Priority Areas**, and in 1974 **Comprehensive Community Action Programmes** were established. Both of these were small scale, locally based attempts at quick fixes with the prime intention of improving the worst areas. Essentially all of these schemes were idea based, but had little coherence in terms of planning, and had insufficient funding. Long-lasting tangible effects were limited.

b) Urban regeneration schemes 1979–92

The Conservative Government under Margaret Thatcher adopted a distinct approach to urban regeneration based on Conservative ideas which emphasised the importance of private sector wealth creation and the reduction in state bureaucracy. Regeneration was concerned initially with physical regeneration and private sector investment, known colloquially as 'Property and Profits'. It was also argued that the benefits of such regeneration would 'trickle down' to the local communities and lead to greater economic and social redevelopment. Three of the most well-known strategies that were employed at the time were Urban Development Corporations (UDCs), Enterprise Zones (EZs) and Inner City Task Forces.

i) Urban Development Corporations
These were responsible for the physical, economic and social regeneration of selected inner city areas with large amounts of derelict and

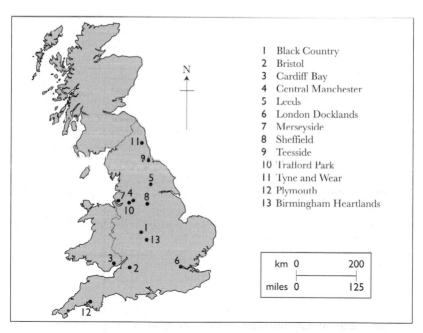

1	Black Country
2	Bristol
3	Cardiff Bay
4	Central Manchester
5	Leeds
6	London Docklands
7	Merseyside
8	Sheffield
9	Teesside
10	Trafford Park
11	Tyne and Wear
12	Plymouth
13	Birmingham Heartlands

Figure 15 Urban Development Corporations

vacant land. They are an example of what is known as Property-led development. They were given planning approval powers, over and above those of the local council, and were encouraged to use public expenditure for the purchase of land, the building of infrastructure, and marketing to attract private investment. The intention was that private investment would be 4 to 5 times greater than that of public investment. The appointed boards of UDCs, mostly made up of people from the local business community, had the power to acquire, reclaim and service land prior to private sector involvement and to provide financial incentives to attract private investors. In 1981, two UDCs were established – the London Docklands (perhaps the most well-known of all UDCs – see case study), and on Merseyside. Eleven others followed, such as the Lower Don Valley in Sheffield, Birmingham Heartlands, Trafford Park, Manchester and Cardiff Bay (Figure 15).

By 1993, UDCs accounted for nearly 40% of all urban regeneration policy expenditure. Over £12 billion of private sector investment had been attracted along with £4 billion from the public sector . They had built or refurbished 35,000 housing units, and created 190,000 jobs (Figure 16).

Some writers have argued that this sum of new employment was inadequate. There were, however, two more significant criticisms.

		expenditure (£ millions)		Lifetime targets		
Location	date started	92–3	95–6	Land reclaimed (hectares)	Housing (units)	Jobs
London Docklands	1981	293.9	88	846.5	24036	75458
Merseyside	1981	42.1	34	384.0	3544	23357
Trafford Park	1987	61.3	29.7	400.6	3774	21440
Black Country	1987	68.0	36.6	525.3	1403	10212
Teeside	1987	34.5	47.5	210.8	311	25618
Tyne and Wear	1987	50.2	43.5	517.7	4842	34043
Central Manchester	1988	20.5	13.7	60.0	661	4590
Cardiff Bay	1988			250.0	950	2200
Leeds	1988	9.6		35.3	2581	5074
Sheffield	1988	15.9	11.6	68.0	561	8369
Bristol	1989	20.4	8.7	259.6	0	17616
Birmingham Heartlands	1992	5.0	11.7	129.1	878	5983
Plymouth	1993	n/a	10.6	12.7	93	491

Figure 16 UDCs – expenditure and targets

Firstly, they were too dependent on property speculation and they lost huge sums of money through the compulsory purchase of land whose value subsequently fell. Secondly, they dramatically reduced the power of local authorities by removing democratic accountability. Local people often complained that they had no involvement in the developments that were taking place. Indeed, there were some examples, particularly in the London Docklands where the locals felt physically and socially excluded by prestigious new housing and high-technology office developments.

ii) Enterprise Zones (EZs)

These were small areas of derelict or vacant land designated to stimulate economic activity by lifting financial burdens and administrative controls. The size of the land varied from 50 to 400 acres, and by the end of the scheme 29 EZs had been established. The planning regime was simplified, companies did not have to pay local business property taxes and investors could offset capital expenditure on industrial and commercial property development against tax. Expenditure is hard to estimate because in these areas the policy was based more on the government choosing not to collect certain taxes rather than on direct public expenditure. Not all the EZs that were created were in inner city areas, and some were established in small towns, for example Corby, where the traditional industry of steel had declined greatly.

There was also some overlap with the UDCs where some of their land was designated as an EZ as well. For example, both the London Docklands and the Lower Don Valley had EZs designated within them. The largest single office development built in the UK at Canary Wharf was in an EZ, and much of the £2 billion private sector investment was partly attracted by EZ tax incentives.

All the EZs were designed to last for a period of ten years, after which the incentives no longer applied. Questions have arisen over how many new jobs were in fact created, and the effect they had on the surrounding area. Firms establishing in the EZs often moved from just outside, in order to make use of the concessions offered, thus giving rise to little new employment. The areas immediately outside of the EZ were at a disadvantage; they had none of the inducements of the land just 100 metres away. Such areas often became derelict themselves, creating a 'shadow effect'. Many EZs failed to attract innovative firms, and one estimate was that each job created actually cost national taxpayers £150,000.

iii) Inner City Task Forces

These were launched in 1986. They consisted of small teams of civil servants who acted as 'think-tanks' to saturate deprived communities with aid and grants. Two such areas included the St Paul's district of Bristol, and Moss Side in Manchester. Since that time, they have created over 48,000 jobs, provided over 200,000 training places, assisted 67,000 businesses to varying degrees and supported over 50,000 educational programmes. They were essentially temporary in nature, and worked closely with key partners in the designated area to ensure that continued regeneration was sustained. However, there was some criticism that they cut across the work of local councils, and were not as popular as central government made out.

They did however begin the move towards 'partnerships' between all sectors of a community. They worked not only towards improving the economic environment, but also towards environmental and recreational developments. Examples of their work include the Everton Park development, various sports centres and the Garden Festival in Liverpool. The Task Force in Handsworth in Birmingham created 800 new jobs, and 900 training places. They were in some places the catalyst towards the gentrification of many individual houses in inner city areas.

c) Urban regeneration schemes 1993–97

Urban Development Corporations and Enterprise Zones continued to exist into the 1990s but they were all scheduled to finish their work during this decade. In 1992 the Conservative Government revised the nature of their policies of urban regeneration. The revision came about due to two main criticisms. Firstly, that local governments and communities had not been allowed to play a full role in the development and application of policy. Secondly, that the wide range of policies had not been very well coordinated. During their long period in power, the Conservatives had lost a large number of by-elections and local council seats. Their centralised way of running urban regeneration schemes may have been one of the factors responsible for their losses at the ballot box.

i) City Challenge Partnerships

These represented a major switch of funding mechanisms towards competitive bidding. Local government had to think of imaginative projects but also had to form partnerships in their local inner city area with the private sector and the local communities. The partnership then had to submit a five year plan to central government in competition with other inner city areas. The most successful schemes combined social aims with economic and environmental outcomes. By 1993, over 30 City Challenge Partnerships had been established, with another 20+ bids having been unsuccessful at that stage. By the end of the year these Partnerships accounted for over 20% of inner city expenditure on regeneration. Figure 17 illustrates the range of areas that received funding.

The City Challenge initiative was designed to address some of the weaknesses of the earlier regeneration schemes. The participating

Bidding round	Successful bidders
1	Bradford, Dearne Valley, Lewisham, Liverpool, Manchester, Middlesbrough, Newcastle, Nottingham, Tower Hamlets, The Wirral, Wolverhampton.
2	Barnsley, Birmingham, Blackburn, Bolton, Brent, Derby, Hackney, Hartlepool, Kirklees, Lambeth, Leicester, Newham, North Tyneside, Sandwell, Sefton, Stockton on Tees, Sunderland, Walsall, Wigan.

Figure 17 Successful City Challenge Partnerships

organisations, the Partners, were better coordinated and more involved. This particularly applied to the residents of the area and the local council. Separate schemes and initiatives operating in the same area, as had happened before, were not allowed – the various strands of the projects had to work together. Many earlier initiatives had concentrated on improving buildings, whereas City Challenge gave equal importance to buildings, people and values. Cooperation between local authorities and private and public groups, some of which were voluntary, was prioritised.

All the City Challenge areas suffered from high unemployment, both youth and long term, a low skills base, poor levels of educational attainment, environmental deterioration, increasing areas of derelict land, and growing commercial property vacancy. Public sector housing was deteriorating in almost all the City Challenge areas due to a combination of poor initial design and inadequate maintenance. The population of these areas usually had a higher than national average incidence of health care problems, high levels of personal crime and fear of crime, a high proportion of single parent families and households dependent on Social Security.

Some City Challenge areas had large ethnic minorities. In Batley, for example, only 40% of the male ethnic population was employed compared with 70% of the white population. In Wolverhampton, over 80% of the ethnic population was in unskilled manual jobs, compared with less than 50% of the white population.

The priorities of the different City Challenge areas also varied. In Liverpool, priority was given to environmental improvement, in Wolverhampton a Science Park formed the centrepiece of the project. In Hulme, Manchester, housing improvement was the main focus.

Overall, the aspect of bidding for funds was deemed to be a success. It is believed that City Challenge Partnerships improved the overall quality of proposals and encouraged new thinking and more imaginative ideas. The private sector, in particular, found the competitive principle attractive and argued that competition had encouraged local authorities to try to suggest solutions as well as identifying problems.

However, the competitive aspect was criticised by others. They argued that the basis for the allocation of large sums of money should not have been based upon competition, but upon need. In some cases, the competition set neighbouring authorities against each other, when they could have worked together. It is rare, for example, for the limits of disadvantaged areas to coincide conveniently at an administrative boundary. The policy that all successful bidders should receive exactly the same sum of money, irrespective of size of need, was also criticised. Finally, competing authorities were not given clear information on the criteria on which their application was to be judged – for some it was a stab in the dark.

The Conservative Government was able by 1997 to publish statistics pointing towards the success of City Challenge Partnerships. Over 40,000 houses had been improved, 53,000 jobs were created, nearly 2000 hectares of derelict land had been reclaimed, and over 3000 new businesses had been established.

ii) The Single Regeneration Budget (SRB)

One of the major criticisms of earlier urban regeneration schemes was that there had been too many initiatives going on at the same time, with little cooperation between them. The range of projects was too fragmented and confusing. The SRB was introduced to pull together more than 20 different sources of regeneration funding under one umbrella organisation administered by the Department for the Environment.

As with the City Challenge Partnerships, funds were decided and allocated by competition. All local authorities had to submit regeneration proposals, but only some were successful and awarded funding. It was the intention that better coordination would result, and that the policies would be more responsive to the particular needs of individual inner city areas. One criticism that was made, however, was that funding again did not match need, it was more a response to the quality of the bid. So, areas which had previously received generous funding, such as parts of Nottingham and Leicester, now received much less, whereas perhaps less needy areas, such as parts of Stoke on Trent received more, following a very successful submission.

iii) European Regional Development Fund

Since 1992, certain parts of the UK have been eligible for money for regeneration from the European Regional Development Fund, and this has become an increasingly important source of finance for such schemes. The European Regional Development Fund classifies those regions of Europe that are eligible for support into Objective 1 and Objective 2 categories.

Objective 1 regions have an annual Gross Domestic Product (GDP) that is below 75% of the European average. In 1993, Liverpool became the first area in the UK to qualify for this status, and consequently has received considerable sums of money for regeneration schemes. More areas now qualify, including a large part of South Yorkshire (Sheffield, Barnsley, Rotherham and Doncaster).

Objective 2 regions are those areas which are experiencing industrial decline, and large areas of the UK's inner cities have been classified as such. However, the impact of the funding has yet to be identified.

d) Urban regeneration schemes 1997–2001

The incoming Labour Government inherited many of the schemes referred to above, and largely supported their aims and methods with a number of modifications. In 1997, the government announced that the **Single Regeneration Budget Challenge Fund** (clearly an amalgamation of two of the previous schemes) would place a greater emphasis on local priorities and local involvement. The priorities for expenditure would be tackling unemployment, crime and poor housing, with an emphasis on an area's greatest need.

Also in 1997, a new Task Force was announced with the aim of revitalising the former coalfield communities. In terms of urban regeneration, **Regional Development Agencies** (RDAs) have been given the task of coordinating economic development, especially in terms of attracting investment and helping small businesses. As with any form of state intervention, time is needed to judge their effectiveness.

Finally, as the twentieth century drew to a close, a new rash of government and quasi non governmental (QUANGO) initiatives began to emerge all aimed at improving the same type of area. In education, the **Education Action Zones (EAZs)** were created, in health **Health Action Zones**, and the century ended with a range of **Millennium schemes**, many of which were based in former derelict inner city areas. These included the new Welsh National Stadium in Cardiff, and the infamous Millennium Dome in the London Docklands.

Case study: The London Docklands

The London Docklands is an area of urban regeneration stretching down stream from London Bridge through Wapping, Limehouse, the Isle of Dogs, Surrey Docks and the Royal Docks. This area was, until the 1960s, the leading port of the UK, but it suffered major decline as shipping switched to the use of both larger vessels and the container based system. New and expanded ports were established around the country, at places

a Allocating the funds %

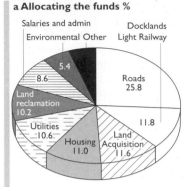

- Salaries and admin
- Environmental Other
- Docklands Light Railway
- 5.4
- 8.6
- Land reclamation 10.2
- Roads 25.8
- Utilities 10.6
- Housing 11.0
- Land Acquisition 11.6
- 11.8

b The Jobs balance sheet

Total jobs attached	41,421
Transfers from elsewhere	24,862
New jobs created	16,862
Jobs lost in Docklands	20,532
Net change of jobs in Dockland	3,670

c Employment profile trends (%)

1981

1 Other manufacturing 29.0

2 Transport and communications 20.8

3 Distribution, hotels etc. 15.5

4 Other services 10.5

Total jobs 27 213

Jobs attracted 1981-91

1 Banking, finance and business services 23.7

2 Other manufacturing 19.2

3 Distribution etc 14.7

4 Construction 14.0

Total jobs 41 421

d Unemployment

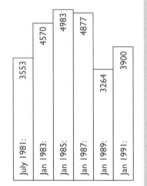

- July 1981: 3553
- Jan 1983: 4570
- Jan 1985: 4983
- Jan 1987: 4877
- Jan 1989: 3264
- Jan 1991: 3900

e Housing completions to March 1992

- 804
- 2 031
- 12 385

■ Private development
▦ Housing Association
□ Local Authority

f Spending on roads (£ million)

Govt. spending on East London roads to improve Docklands access: £1.2 billion

g Social housing (retail & joint equity) (£ million)

— New units
— Refurbishment

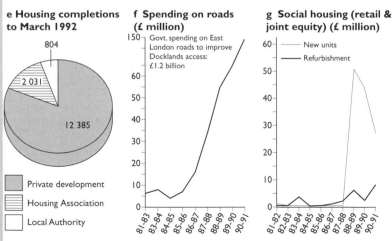

Figure 18 Reviewing the LDDC performance, 1981–91

such as Gravesend, Tilbury, Felixstowe and Dover, causing the decline of London as a port, and huge dereliction of the docks.

The Conservative Government set up the first Urban Development Corporation, the London Docklands Development Corporation (LDDC) in 1981. With government grants, private investment and the sale of reclaimed land to developers, together with improvements to the infrastructure such as roads and a new Light Railway, the economy of the area has been transformed. A new short take-off and landing (STOL) airport, (London City airport), has been built with links to other European cities such as Paris and Frankfurt. The area has developed private housing, offices, shopping, hotels and leisure facilities with over 700 new firms having located there (Figure 18).

These industries are largely service-based activities such as financial and business services, leisure, restaurants, and catering organisations. Several printing and publishing organisations relocated to the area, particularly national newspapers such as the Sun, the Daily Telegraph and Sunday Telegraph. High technology industries, media-based industries such as television production companies and film companies have also sought new prestigious locations there.

Although the LDDC achieved great economic success, it also achieved notoriety for its failure to involve the local community in a range of ways. Consultation with local councils was minimal, the local residents were largely priced out of the housing market by the new developments which took place. The nature of the employment created was not suited to the skills of the former dockland workers, and few community facilities were provided for the existing residents. In many ways, the domineering strategies used by the LDDC became the main reason for the changes in approach that took place in the 1990s in urban regeneration policies.

In 1998, the LDDC ceased to exist. Some of its responsibilities were handed over to the local councils of Newham, Southwark and Tower Hamlets. Others were given to the British Waterways Board, and to City Challenge Partnerships. At its demise the LDDC was able to claim the following successes during its 17 year existence:

- £7.2 billion private sector investment alongside £1.9 billion invested by the public sector
- 830 hectares of derelict land had been reclaimed
- 145 km of new and improved roads had been built
- the Docklands Light Railway was an economic success
- 24,000 new homes had been constructed
- 2.3 million square metres of commercial and industrial floor space had been created

- 85,000 people now work there in a wide range of activities
- it is a major tourist area, attracting over 2 million visitors a year.

Case Study: The Central Manchester Development Corporation (CMDC)

This is an example of a Development Corporation established later than the LDDC in 1988, where a partnership between the local council and private developers was created. Its aim was to regenerate 200 hectares of land and buildings in the southern sector of Manchester city centre. The area contained decaying warehouses, offices, former mills and contaminated land, unsightly railway viaducts and neglected waterways. The area had been declared a conservation area in 1979.

Some of the buildings were able to be refurbished into a range of activities including housing. For example, in the Whitworth Street district many warehouses were converted and redeveloped to create a village-like atmosphere of more than 1000 household units, pubs, bars, restaurants and shops.

The canals in the area were cleaned, and their banks were improved by the addition of lighting, seats and plants, all in an effort to improve the aesthetics of the area. Consequently, it has become a very popular entertainment-based area for young people.

The CMDC engaged in widespread consultation and formulated a development strategy which complemented the plans of the Manchester City Council. For example, the area of Castlefield which was once an area of disused canals, wharves and warehouses became a mixture of housing (including some luxury apartments), office developments and leisure facilities. The area also developed its tourist potential and now attracts over 2 million visitors a year. Attractions include the world famous tour of Granada Studios, the Manchester Museum of Science and Technology, the GMEX Centre and the Bridgewater Concert Hall complex.

The CMDC was disbanded in 1996, and planning powers have now reverted back to the Manchester City Council.

Case study: The Hulme City Challenge (Manchester)

The Hulme area of Manchester was redeveloped as part of a slum clearance programme in the 1960s with a number of high rise flats. Of the 5500 dwellings, 98% were council owned. Over half of the dwellings were part of a deck access system, with many of the bad design features of prefabricated construction. The area had a low level of families with children, and a disproportionate number of single person households. There were also a high number of single parents, and other people with social difficulties. There was some evidence that the Council had used the area to 'dump' some of its more unfortunate residents.

In 1992, plans were drawn up to build 3000 new homes, with new shopping areas, new roads and community facilities. A more traditional pattern of housing development was designed with streets, squares, two storey houses and low rise flats. By 1995, 50 hectares of land had been reclaimed, the majority of the former deck access flats had been demolished. 600 new homes for rent had been built, and over 400 homes had been improved and refurbished. The main shopping area was totally refurbished, including the addition of an Asda supermarket. A new community centre, The Zion Centre, was also constructed. Crime in the area has been reduced greatly, and there is more of a social mix of people living in the area. The appearance of Hulme had altered radically.

A number of agencies and organisations were responsible for this transformation, including the Guinness Trust, and Bellway Homes. These worked in close collaboration with each other and with Manchester City Council. The company responsible for Manchester Airport also invested capital into the project. The area provides a good example of how the public and private sectors can work together to improve a previously declining, and socially challenging area.

Case study: The Grainger Town Regeneration Project, Newcastle upon Tyne

During the early part of the 1990s the political attitudes towards regeneration changed. Politicians of all parties had come to see the benefits of partnership between the various tiers of government and the other bodies working to achieve economic and social improvements.

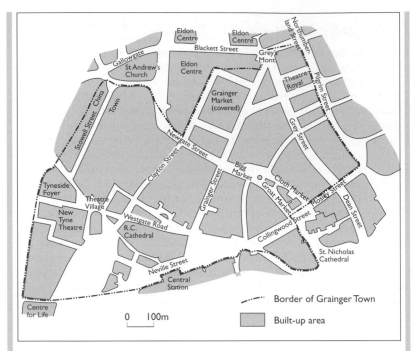

Figure 19 Grainger Town

In 1994, some of the City Challenge Partnerships were put in the overall control of English Partnerships, an organisation set up by central government. The aim of English Partnerships was to secure the regeneration of areas of need through the reclamation and redevelopment of land and buildings. Whilst it concentrated on land and buildings, it also had to operate within the wider regeneration framework, and work with local and regional partners aiming to tackle the problems of an area as a whole. One such area where English Partnerships played a major role was in the Grainger Town area of Newcastle upon Tyne.

Grainger Town covers 30 hectares of land in the southern part of Newcastle's city centre (Figure 19). It extends from Stowell Street in the west to Pilgrim Street in the east, from Blackett Street in the north to Neville Street in the south. Within this area, there is a fine collection of late Georgian and early Victorian classic buildings dating back to the 1820s. Over 60% of the buildings are listed, and 20% have a Grade 1 status.

By the mid 1990s, Grainger Town had become an area of office, retail, residential, leisure and cultural uses. Parts of the area, Bigg Market, Stowell Street and The Theatre Village, had developed distinctive characters. Despite this the area had fallen victim to the changes in retail and commercial activities, mainly the movement to modern out-of-town locations. The area's economic base was being eroded, and the fabric of the buildings was beginning to fall into disrepair. A large area of commercial floor space was unoccupied (93,000 square metres), and several of the listed buildings were classified as being at risk by English Heritage. Its public spaces were of poor quality and there were parking and traffic problems.

English Partnerships' strategy was to bring new vitality to the area by enhancing the qualities the area already possessed. During 1995 and 1996 they invested £6 million in Grainger Town projects. One of these was the development of the Tyneside Foyer. This was set up and operated by the Salvation Army and was a residential and training centre for young homeless and unemployed people. Newcastle City Council and English Heritage invested over £1 million in the repair and re-use of vacant buildings, many of which were listed.

In the future, a huge £120 million regeneration programme will be undertaken, including major investment by the private sector, central government and local government. A number of regeneration themes form this strategy:

* To develop existing businesses and to promote the creation of new businesses.
* To improve the quality of traffic management and the quality of the public areas and thereby make the area more attractive to investors.
* To increase the residential population by creating a range of affordable housing for both rent and sale.
* To re-use historic buildings for office, retail, arts and leisure uses.
* To promote the area as a centre for the arts, culture and tourism.
* To market the area successfully for all of the above uses.
  To achieve this mixed-use potential, certain parts of Grainger Town have been targeted for specific land-uses:
* The area immediately south of the Eldon Centre is to be an extension of the retailing area.
* Housing is to be reintroduced in the west of the area, along Clayton Street and Grainger Street.
* The office core is to be strengthened along Grey Street and Collingwood Street.
* Leisure and cultural 'corridors' are to run from St Nicholas' Cathedral along Newgate Street, and in the south west of the area from the new museum, The International Centre for Life, to the Tyne Theatre and Opera House.

A key aspect of all of these strategies is to improve access to and within the area. The Central Railway station lies to the south of the area, and the area is also well served by the Tyneside Metro. The quality of the pedestrian walkways between the various sub-districts also needed to be improved to make the area more attractive.

English Partnerships measured its general success in terms of a number of criteria. The jobs created or safeguarded, the new commercial space made available, the new homes built, the areas of land brought back into use, and the local communities that it supported. As with many such quasi non-governmental organisations aimed at regeneration, its name ceased to exist by the end of 1999.

4 Gentrification

This is a process of housing improvement associated with a change in the neighbourhood composition, when lower income groups are displaced by more affluent people, usually in professional or managerial occupations. It is a process by which the regeneration of inner cities takes place, but it is different from the schemes that have been mentioned before as it is carried out by individuals or groups of individuals, and not by supported bodies.

Gentrification involves the rehabilitation of old houses and streets on an individual basis, but is openly encouraged by other groups such as estate agents, building societies and the local council.

One of the clear positive outcomes is that the social mix of the area is changed in the direction of greater affluence. The purchasing power of the residents becomes greater which leads to a rise in the general level of prosperity in the area. The area becomes dominated by 'yuppies' (young upwardly mobile professionals), with a subsequent increase in the number of bars, restaurants and other higher status services. The very nature of the refurbishment that takes place in each house leads to the creation of employment, such as design, building work, furnishings and decoration, in the area.

There are, however, clear disadvantages of gentrification. Local people on low incomes find it increasingly difficult to purchase houses, as the price of refurbished property rises markedly. Indeed, the size of the privately rented sector diminishes as more properties are sold off. Friction and conflict occurs between the newcomers and the original residents.

Gentrification is taking place in the central parts of a large number of towns and cities in the UK. Examples include Notting Hill and Islington in London, Brindley Place in Birmingham, and the Castlefields area of Manchester. Similar up-market converted dwellings can now be found in the central parts of most towns.

Other areas where there is total redevelopment of a similar nature include the Albert Dock in Liverpool, the Salford Quays in Greater Manchester, the Quayside in Newcastle, and the Marina in Hull. These are all waterfront locations which are particularly attractive and form a focus for the new developments.

The people attracted to these gentrified areas are similar in characteristics. Many are in the 25–35 age range, and are well educated and skilled. They work in high status service sector occupations, notably finance and marketing. They like the leisure and entertainment opportunities offered and the lively atmosphere of the big city. What is more, they have the money with which to enjoy it.

5 Making inner cities safer – the female perspective

Perception has an important role to play in judging a particular place. Whether or not you feel safe in an area is a crucial aspect of being there or travelling to it. The inner cities are increasingly being perceived as threatening and unsafe environments. Any individual or group of society whose movements and activities are constrained by fear may be classified as disadvantaged. They suffer from reduced accessibility and a poorer quality of life. It is often suggested that women perceive themselves to be restricted in this way. What can be done to alleviate these feelings and make women feel safer?

Recent surveys have shown that two-thirds of women are afraid to go out alone at night in urban areas. Many will not use public transport, or venture into city centres in the evening. This perception of fear not only denies women the use of city centres, it is also a significant economic loss to leisure based businesses. For example, in Nottingham it was estimated that the economic loss was £24 million a year. In 1988 the 'Safer Cities Programme' was launched by the government as part of its 'Action for Cities Initiative'. A number of approaches and policies were put into place, which have now become commonplace across the country.

Segregated transport for women:

The idea of public transport provision for women only has been tried in several towns. The first such scheme took place in Bristol following a series of rapes and serious attacks. There are only two buses available, and the service has to be booked in advance. In Bradford, a 'Homerunner' service was introduced for the same target group and shift workers. Several other cities now operate door to door services of this type. They are small scale, and demand is greater than supply. They have been criticised, however, for perpetuating the concept that women must operate under a type of curfew. Allied to this is the formal licensing of mini-cabs in towns and cities across the UK. All forms of private hire vehicles have to be registered and regulated. In

London and Manchester there are special taxi services for women, for example, the Lady Cab service.

Making public transport safer:
A number of towns have imaginative and sensible schemes to make travel by public transport more safe. These include extra staffing and lighting at bus and rail termini, conductors on evening buses, and 'hail and ride' mini-bus services. The major problem is cost, as there are few subsidies available for local authorities to use, and private companies need to make a profit. In Tyne and Wear the trains are shorter at night in order to compress travellers into a smaller space, and reduce the potential for isolation.

Improvement of the street environment:
CCTV surveillance is the main thrust of this, and this is now widespread across the country. It is also enhanced by better quality street lighting, and by emergency alarms being placed strategically around the streets.

However, two types of area still cause some concern, pedestrian subways and multi-storey car parks. The former are being removed in some cities and replaced with surface crossings as redesigning takes place. Multi-storey car parks are more problematic. Better lighting, the provision of women only ground floor sections in them, or women only street parking areas to remove the need to use multi-storey car parks, are suggestions that have been made.

Summary

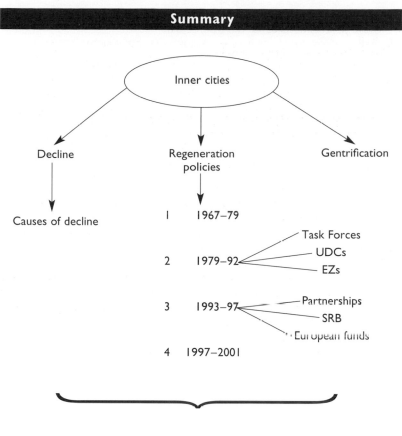

Making inner cities safer

1. Identify the physical signs of decline that many inner city areas demonstrate. How can you tell by walking through such an area that decline is taking place?
2. Summarise the main reasons for the decline of inner city areas.
3. With reference to examples, discuss the impact of Urban Development Corporations on the regeneration of inner cities in the UK.
4. 'Enterprise Zones had little lasting impact on the economic and social regeneration of cities.' Discuss the extent to which you agree with this statement.
5. To what extent were the policies of the urban regeneration schemes

after 1992 different to those before that date? Are there any signs that these policies have been more successful?

6. With reference to examples, discuss the approaches used by City Challenge Partnerships to include and benefit whole communities in inner city areas.

7. Describe the main differences between 'property led redevelopment' and 'gentrification'.

   A word of caution – do not embark on any fieldwork based in inner city areas on your own.

8. Visit an area in your town where gentrification has taken place. Identify the main features of the urban landscape that have changed due to gentrification. Carry out a survey of the origins and employment characteristics of the people who live there.

9. Visit a City Challenge Partnership or Single Regeneration Budget area near where you live. What industries have been located there? What changes have taken place in the housing stock of the area? What are the future plans for further redevelopment in the area?

10. An interesting exercise is to measure the changing perceptions of people who do not live in former inner city areas of a town. Identify an area of your town which you know has undergone marked change and regeneration. Ask people who do not live there what their feelings are about that particular locality – would they live there and why?

4 Suburbanisation and counter-urbanisation

1 Introduction

This chapter examines the two major processes influencing urban growth in the UK in the last 30 years. Towards the end of the twentieth century the influence of suburbanisation, which had been very significant, was declining. In its place came the process of counter-urbanisation as more people left large towns and cities and leap-frogged into the previously unaffected countryside.

2 Suburbanisation

Suburbanisation is the outward growth of urban developments which have engulfed surrounding villages and rural areas. As towns continue to grow, they swallow up the neighbouring rural areas by outward expansion. During the twentieth century, this was facilitated by the growth of public transport systems and the increased use of the private car. Commuters have been able to live some distance away from their place of work and have travelled in along railway lines, bus routes and arterial roads.

To a large extent the towns and cities of the UK demonstrate the effects of past suburbanisation. In the 1930s there were few planning controls and urban growth took place alongside main roads, often called ribbon development. By the 1940s this growth, and the subsequent growth between the 'ribbons' became a source of concern. This led to the creation of Green Belts – areas of open space and low density land use around existing urban areas where further development was strictly controlled.

Since 1950, suburban expansion has increased and has been more planned. The 1950s and 1960s were the period of large scale construction of council housing, for which the only places with sufficient land available were located on the suburban fringe. In the 1970s there followed the move towards home ownership, which in turn led to private housing estates being constructed also on the urban fringe.

Building in these areas allowed people to have more land for gardens, and more public open space compared with housing areas nearer the town centre.

The rising importance of the private car and other forms of road transport gave suburbanisation another source of encouragement. The edge of town became the favoured location for new offices, factories and shopping outlets where there is more land available for car parking and expansion. In a number of cases, the 'strict control' of the Green Belts was ignored or at best modified in the light of changing circumstances.

In the Green Belt of the south east of England, where there is the most pressure for more housing developments, the controls have been generally effective. However, the future growth of the South East is a major issue. A recent report suggested that over 1 million new homes in the region will be needed by 2016.

3 Counter-urbanisation

Counter-urbanisation is the process of people moving away from major urban areas to smaller settlements and rural areas. There is a clear break between the areas of new growth and the urban area from which the people have moved. Consequently, counter-urbanisation does not lead to suburban growth, but rather to the growth of rural areas beyond the main city. The difference between rural and urban areas is diminished as a consequence of this movement.

A number of factors have caused the growth of counter-urbanisation. One is the negative reaction to city life. Many people no longer want the air pollution, dirt and crime of the urban environment. They aspire to the pleasant, quiet and clean environment of the countryside. Here, land and house prices are cheaper. Higher personal car ownership and greater affluence allow people to commute to their place of work. Indeed, many sources of employment have followed suit and have moved to rural areas as well. Between 1981 and 1996, rural areas gained more than one million jobs. Improvements in technology have allowed this to happen – there is more freedom of location. Even on an individual basis, one individual working from a home computer work station can access the same global system as a person in an office block in the centre of a city.

In addition to these factors, there are the more recent trends of the rising demand for second homes and earlier retirement. The former is a direct consequence of rising levels of affluence, as well as the reduced amount of time that workers need to be in the office. Alongside this is the need within rural areas to raise money. Agriculture is currently facing many economic difficulties, and one straightforward way to raise money is to sell unwanted land and buildings.

Counter-urbanisation affects the layout of rural settlements. Modern housing estates are built on the edges of small settlements, with small industrial units being sited on the main roads leading into the settlement. Former open areas are built on, old properties are converted and modernised, and some agricultural buildings are redeveloped as homes. As with gentrified areas within the inner cities, there is tension between the newcomers and the locals.

One of the main areas of conflict is that local services often close down despite the influx of new people. Bus services to many rural communities have disappeared, schools and post offices have closed down, and churches have closed as more and more parishes are amalgamated into larger units. The main reason for this is that the newcomers have the wealth and the mobility to continue to use the urban services some distance away.

Case study: The effects of counter-urbanisation – St Ives, Cambridgeshire

The small town of St Ives in Cambridgeshire is about 65 miles north of London. It lies on the A1123 road three miles east of Huntingdon and seven miles north west of Cambridge just off the main trunk road A14. The town is very close to both the A1 trunk road and the main East Coast railway line. Regular trains to London make the area very accessible (Figure 20).

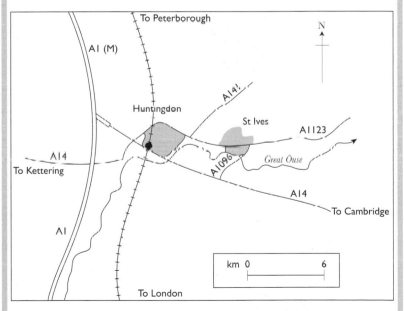

Figure 20 Location of St Ives, Cambridgeshire

The surrounding rural area is mainly farmland. However, in recent years there have been considerable new housing developments on the periphery of the small town. There has also been a substantial amount of new exclusive apartment building within the heart of the town, and particularly on the south bank of the Great Ouse river.

The population structure of the town is changing. Whilst one section of the community is ageing, another part is becoming more youthful. A large proportion of the working population is now employed outside the town. In particular, there has been a substantial influx of people from in and around London who prefer commuting to living in the city. Housing in the area is affordable and a sustained boom in demand for property has been the result. People in St Ives have higher incomes and higher standards of living than in other parts of the UK. With these higher incomes, they are able to afford the higher travel costs to London on the railway. Recently retired people are also moving into the area and their impact is also noticeable in the increased demand for bungalows and small riverside apartment blocks.

Commuting to London has increased during the 1990s. The main line to London has been electrified, and journey times are much reduced. The station at Huntingdon is about 50 minutes from Kings Cross in central London. It is now estimated that 25% of St Ives' working population commute to London each day. For many of these it is a decision whether to pay high housing costs in London and be closer to work, or to have a rural/small town environment in which to live and travel from each day.

While prosperity in the town has been increasing for some of the elderly who own their own property and for families who have moved out of London, for others there is a different picture. There is an increasing gap between those who can afford the rising cost of housing and commuting, and those on low wages, such as farm workers, or on part-time wages or youth training schemes. For these latter groups, the cost of housing is beyond their means. Clearly, there is a demand for low cost housing for young local families, but there are few organisations or builders who are prepared to provide it.

St Ives may well be close to a railway station at Huntingdon, and have a high car ownership amongst its population, but as with other rural areas its bus services are poor. The service to the town is infrequent, although it is better than many others as it lies on more or less a direct route between Cambridge and Huntingdon. Bus transport is available during priority times, namely, the start and end of the school day and market days.

The town is affected by trends affecting the whole area. The area lies close to two of the main North–South arterial routeways – the A1 and the East Coast Main Line. Commuters are attracted to the town for two main reasons – the ease of communication to London and the quality of life in the small rural town. Pressure to increase the housing stock in the area is increasing, fuelled by demand from commuters. For builders there is great potential for business. There is some resistance to the building of more homes from the local residents, but many of these are relatively new to the area themselves and do not want their newly chosen environment changed.

It is unlikely that additional house construction will not take place, demand is too great. However, developers will be encouraged to make sure that the new developments blend in as much as possible with the current urban landscape. There will need to be an acceptable density of buildings, use of appropriate construction materials, provision of sufficient open space, preservation of vistas, and good and appropriate provision of street furniture (road signs, seating, lampposts etc.). Any further development must make a positive contribution to the overall character of the area.

Summary

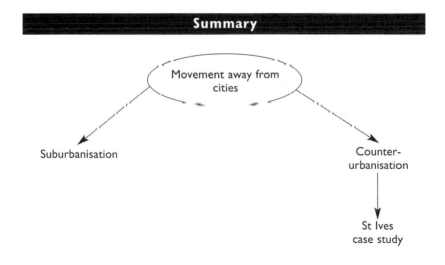

Questions

1. What is the difference between suburbanisation and counter-urbanisation?
2. What are the main factors contributing to the increase in counter-urbanisation in the UK today?
3.
   a Draw up a table to show the advantages and disadvantages of living in (i) St Ives and (ii) London.
   b How will this table vary for people of differing age or family status?
   c Which of the two areas would you prefer to live in? Justify your answer.
4. 'If small rural towns and villages are to survive in the UK, we need to ensure that they remain communities for all of their population, not just the wealthy.' Discuss the extent to which you agree with this statement.
5. Visit a small town or village where counter-urbanisation is taking place. Carry out a survey of the socio-economic characteristics of the population. Find out age structures, places of employment, means of travel to work, and shopping destinations.
6. Imagine a new housing development is planned for the area where you live. Devise a design checklist of the main features that the new housing development must have.
7. Imagine you are considering altering the exterior of your own house. You could be changing any external detail – the paintwork, the building itself, the garden, the garden furniture. Undertake a design assessment of the effect of the proposed change. How will it affect the overall features of the property? Will the change be out of character with the rest of the building, or out of character with the neighbouring properties? Will the change make a positive contribution to the character of the area?

5 Managing urban transport

1 Introduction

This chapter examines the causes of urban transport problems within the UK, in terms of traffic movement, and also in terms of pollution. The variety of proposals to solve these problems are then reviewed. The progressive outward spread of houses into the suburbs and small towns and villages, together with the continued concentration of jobs in the central parts of cities continue to generate powerful morning and evening surges of commuters. These surges are at their most extreme in London, but also exist in most other large towns and cities across the UK. They take place along roads (private cars and commercial buses) and along railway networks. In addition to these movements, other flows for shopping, entertainment and other commercial services (for example, lorries and vans) add to the overall problems of mass transportation. It is generally accepted that the current roads network of the UK cannot cope. No matter how much money is spent on transport infrastructure, traffic jams, railway overcrowding, and parking problems get progressively worse.

This realisation is not new. The first London underground line was opened in 1863, and the first deep tube electric railway in 1890. These were built to overcome the urban transport problems in London at that time. Interestingly, the average speed along the Underground in 1890 was 24 km/hour, the same as the average speed of central London tube trains in 1995. In 1963, the Buchanan Report entitled *Traffic in Towns* showed that the private car was clogging up the central parts of cities. Indeed, this report concluded that the only effective way to control car usage was through 'good cheap public transport.'

However, despite mounting problems, and evidence of worse to come, government policy in the UK has continued to favour private road transport. Government figures still demonstrate the unabated expansion of roads, road traffic and progressively heavier goods vehicles. Alongside this there has been relatively slow growth in railway usage. The number of people carried on UK railways has increased, particularly in the London region, but this has been accompanied by problems of poor rolling stock, escalating fares, accidents and horrendous accounts of travel. It is difficult to persuade people to abandon their cars.

Many authors have called for a coordinated and balanced public transport policy. As further road building is likely to release suppressed demand and hence quickly fill up the extra capacity (as in the infamous case of the M25), greater emphasis should be placed on upgrading the public transport system. Finding a solution to the problem of urban transport has exercised town planners and traffic consultants for many years.

2 How and why is urban traffic increasing?

Car ownership is increasing throughout the world. Globally it is anticipated that the total number of motor vehicles will be over 800 million in 2010. Most of these will be concentrated in the MEDCs, and in the urban areas within these. Within the UK, over 20% of households own two or more cars. There are several reasons for this growth.

1. **A high and growing urban working population:**
   A high proportion of the employed work in the major urban areas of the country but live in rural or suburban areas. These people continue to make regular journeys to and from their home by both road and rail. However, there are changes taking place in this pattern. Many commuter journeys now take place between one suburb and another, rather than suburb to town centre. Most public transport systems were developed to travel from suburb to town centre, rather than across town, and so suburb to suburb journeys have to be undertaken by private car. Consequently, some suburban roads can be as congested as those in the centre.
   As suburbanisation and counter-urbanisation takes place, the cost of expanding public transport networks becomes prohibitive. It becomes more and more difficult therefore to encourage people away from what is to them the most convenient form of transport – the car.
2. **Further economic growth:**
   Commuting is not the only reason for more vehicles being on the roads. Economic growth in retailing and other consumer services has led to more service vehicles (including supermarket lorries and the notorious white van) being on urban roads. It is an alarming thought that freight traffic, such as delivery vans, is likely to increase as e-commerce becomes more important in retailing.

3. **The growth in urban incomes:**
   Earnings in urban areas are usually higher than in rural areas, and these higher incomes have led to a rise in car ownership. The rise in incomes has been faster than the relative rise in car prices, leading to the rise in multiple car ownership in many families.

4. **The growth in the number of journeys:**
   As the number of cars owned by people increases, so does the number of journeys that people make in them. There is also a consequent fall in the use of public transport. In addition, research in the USA has suggested that not only does the number of journeys increase with car ownership, but so does the distance travelled. Many of these extra journeys are for leisure purposes.

3 Atmospheric traffic pollution in urban areas

In urban areas road traffic is the major source of atmospheric particulates. These are constituents of the atmosphere which are solids rather than gases. They derive mainly from vehicle exhausts, particularly those burning diesel fuel. They have adverse effects on human health, especially when there are also large quantities of the gas ozone at ground levels. Both of these forms of pollution cause problems such as bronchial complaints, asthma and eye irritation.

Asthma is a growing problem within the UK. Low altitude ozone and nitrogen oxides irritate the lungs and cause breathing problems for asthma sufferers. It is now estimated that there are over 3 million people who suffer from the complaint, including one in ten children. As with many other illnesses, the effect in terms of working days lost is massive, and is estimated at 6 million a year.

Other pollutants are emitted by vehicle exhausts. Nitrogen oxides, hydrocarbons and lead are also dispersed into the atmosphere, although the amount of lead is steadily decreasing with the widespread use of unleaded fuel. Under strong sunlight a photochemical process occurs which produces low altitude ozone. Where there is little or no wind, a haze hangs over the urban area, sometimes accompanied by a smell.

Catalytic converters have been introduced into all new cars in an attempt to reduce this problem. They are designed to remove nitrogen oxides, carbon monoxide and any unburnt hydrocarbons from an exhaust. However, to be effective they must have a hot engine (which with many small journeys to the shops or school does not always occur), and they also increase the amount of carbon dioxide actually emitted.

4 Possible solutions to urban transport problems

There are four main approaches to dealing with urban transport problems.

1. **The introduction of new road schemes that restrict access to certain areas:**
   London has had chronic road traffic problems for many years. In the 1970s and 1980s new ring and radial routes were advocated as solutions. The M25 was completed during this time as the new London Orbital motorway, but as stated earlier all this appeared to do was to unlock the potential for further cars on the road. There are now plans to increase the size of this motorway in response to demand, or even to build a parallel relief motorway. Many of the plans for new radial routes were abandoned in 1990, although some work was completed, for example to the A40(M) Westway link.
   On a smaller scale, the creation of bus lanes, with added priority at junctions, is viewed as being an effective way of encouraging public transport use as well as decreasing car traffic. However, the extension of this into a bus lane on the M4 has proved to be both unsuccessful and unpopular. Once again in London, there are suggestions for blocking off areas in the centre to private motorists and/or charging tolls for those choosing to drive through the centre of the city.

2. **The introduction of road traffic management schemes:**
   Many provincial cities suffer from severe traffic congestion too. For them the option of a new ring road or new arterial routes is not available. For towns such as Oxford, bypasses and inner ring roads already exist, in some cases formed by the amalgamation and upgrading of existing routes. But, despite these measures traffic problems continue.
   The following are some of the strategies that are being introduced in many of these smaller towns and cities:
   Severe on-street parking controls, and provision of expensive multi-storey parking.
   Restrictions on vehicular movement, for example, pedestrianisation of large areas of the centres.
   One way systems and traffic calming measures.
   Encouragement of usage of public transport, for example, Park and Ride schemes.

3. **The integration and streamlining of present public transport systems:**
   As long as 30 years ago, Passenger Transport Authorities were set up to run and maintain efficient integrated public transport within their areas. In the case of Merseyside, the Authority, under the name Merseytravel, is responsible for the Mersey tunnels, the Mersey ferries, Merseyrail and the Merseytravel bus services. It operates in a difficult geographical area, serving the Wirral peninsula as well as the county of Merseyside to the east of the Mersey estuary.
   The key to the public transport system is Merseyrail. One third of the area's population lives within 1 km of a Merseyrail station and the system is intensively used for public access to the city centre. There are three main lines, the Wirral line that links Liverpool city centre with New Brighton, West Kirby and Hooton; the Northern line that serves Kirby,

Ormskirk and Southport; and the City line to Wigan and Crewe. There are constant new initiatives, such as new stations (for example, at Whiston), updating of electrified lines, and a centralised control system. Commercial bus companies operate the bus services, with some authority provision for the disabled. Two ferry routes cross the Mersey, from Liverpool to Birkenhead and from Liverpool to Wallasey. However, they operate at a slight loss. Both Mersey tunnels are operated by Merseytravel, and with just over 1 million vehicles passing through manage a small profit.

4. **The introduction of new mass transit systems:**
   These can be used to provide a new level of low cost public transport from the suburbs to the city centre. Two recent examples include the Supertram in Sheffield and the Metrolink in Manchester.
   It has taken a number of years for UK traffic managers to recognise the benefits of modern electrified tram systems on urban movement. They did not have to look far away to see these benefits. In Germany, France, the Netherlands and Switzerland light mass transit systems based on trams have eased traffic congestion and provided an effective public transport system for years.

Phase 1 of the Manchester Metrolink opened in 1992, and there have already been some extensions to the network, for example to the Salford Quays and Trafford Park (Figure 21). The initial link ran

Figure 21 The Manchester Metrolink

from Bury in the north to Altrincham in the south serving 18 stations on the conventional rail network as well as 6 street level stations in the city centre. Interchange facilities are provided at Manchester's main-line railway stations, Piccadilly and Victoria. The Metrolink operates at intervals of 5 minutes during peak periods, and 12 to 15 minutes during less busy periods. During construction there were inevitable problems of disruption during the laying of tracks, but the longer term benefits are now becoming apparent. In the early years of the project, the fleet of 24 trams carried more than 9 million passengers, nearly twice the number predicted.

Case study: Commuting by rail into London

The problems associated with road traffic in London have been referred to above, but commuting by rail presents different problems.

Commuting into London is undertaken by two separate rail networks. One of them focusses on the main line termini both north and south of the river. To cross or move through London one is most likely to make use of the London Underground system. Consequently, many people have to change systems, and this interchange may take five to ten minutes moving in crowded underpasses and passageways and on to equally crowded platforms.

A key factor in the decision to buy or rent a dwelling is the proximity to a direct railway line to a person's place of employment. There are three elements to the journey to work, from home to the station, station to station including any change of trains where necessary, and access from station to work. Research has shown that journeys by rail in the London area can take between 30 and 60 minutes to cover 20 km. It is easy to see therefore how the commuting journey can take over 1 hour each way each day.

Proposed new links have been considered, but the lengthy amount of completion time and escalating costs of the construction of the recent extension to the Jubilee Line have highlighted the difficulties of these investments. London still has problems where crossing the River Thames in a north–south direction is involved. The Thames-Link line has been developed, which reinstated a disused connection between Farringdon and Holborn, but movement along it in its central section is far from rapid.

With this mind, London Underground have announced proposals to extend the East London line both to the north and the south (Figure 22). The existing East London line is short in length but geographically important, in that it is one of a few cross-river rail links in the capital. To the north there are plans

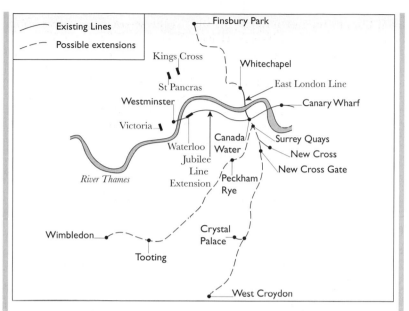

Figure 22 Extension to the East London line

to connect Whitechapel with Railtrack's North London Line and eventually to Finsbury Park station. Interestingly, this will provide Hackney, one of the most populated boroughs in London, with its first Underground line. To the south there are two current proposals: one from Surrey Quays to Wimbledon; the other from New Cross Gate to Crystal Palace and West Croydon. It is suggested that the key benefits of this scheme are:

*   to provide easier access to the Underground for more people in north-east and south London
*   to provide significantly quicker journeys to the City and the Docklands
*   to reduce traffic congestion on key roads, the A10, A205 and A23
*   to provide more opportunities for orbital journeys, thus taking pressure from the central London stations.

Additional benefits would be to encourage more use of public transport at the expense of the private car, thereby reducing air pollution. Also, as existing disused railway routes could be brought back into use, there would be limited disruption during construction.

Summary

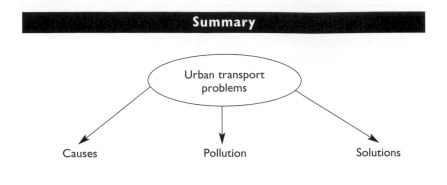

Questions

1. Outline the main causes of the increase in urban traffic within the UK in the last 20 years.

2. Discuss some of the solutions that have been suggested for urban road traffic problems.

3.
  a Why does air quality in urban areas differ from that of surrounding rural areas?
  b Outline some of the effects of poor air quality on people.

4. 'Urban transport problems can only be solved by a coherent public transport policy. Central government should take the lead in the formulation of such a policy.'
Discuss the extent to which you agree with this statement.

5. Carry out a survey of the journey to work by people in your area. How much time do they spend travelling, what distance do they move, and at what cost?

6. Carry out a traffic survey along one or more major commuter routes into your local town or city. Calculate average numbers of vehicles passing per hour, and average speeds at different times of the day.

7. Investigate the range of road traffic management schemes that are used by the local authority where you live. Are there, for example, any restricted parking areas, or a Park and Ride scheme? How effective are they? Does the price of car parking vary within the town centre?

8. Investigate the systems by which the quality of air is measured in your area. What elements of air quality are measured and monitored? How have the results varied within the last few years? In which parts of the urban area are air quality levels (i) particularly good, and (ii) very poor?

References

Chaffey, J. (1994) *A New View of Britain,* Hodder and Stoughton.

Prosser, R, (1995) *Managing Environmental Systems,* Nelson.

Prosser, R. (1992) *Human Systems and the Environment,* Nelson.

Raw, M. (1993) *Manufacturing Industry: the Impact of Change,* Collins.

Skinner et al. (2000) *The Complete A–Z Geography Handbook,* Hodder and Stoughton.

Appendix

Developing extended prose and essay writing skills

These will produce one of the most difficult aspects of the examination paper, but many students will also find this to be true – this is an opportunity for the student to demonstrate how good he/she can be.

There is a set procedure to writing pieces of extended prose. First of all you must have a plan of what you are going to write in your head, or on paper, before you start. All pieces of extended prose must have a beginning (introduction), a middle (argument) and an end (conclusion).

The introduction:

This must be there, but it does not have to be too long. It can be only one, or a few, sentences. It could provide a definition of terms given in the question, or it could set the scene for the argument to follow, or it could be a brief statement of an idea/concept/viewpoint that you are going to develop in the main body of your answer.

The argument:

This will form the main element of your answer, and so will appear as a series of paragraphs. It is better if each paragraph develops one point only, but fully. Try to avoid paragraphs which list information without any depth or breadth in your answer. Also avoid answers where you put down all you know about a particular topic without any link to the actual question set. Make good use of all examples – name real places (which could be local to you). Make them count by giving accurate detail which applies to the examples specifically, rather than to 'anytown' or 'anyplace'.

The conclusion:

In an extended prose answer the conclusion should not be too long. Make sure it reiterates the main points stated in the introduction, but now supported by the evidence and facts given in the argument.

Should you produce plans of extended prose in the examination?
If you produce a plan at all, it must be brief, taking only 2–3 minutes to write, and it is suggested that it is not completed on the examination paper itself, but on a spare piece of paper. The plan must reflect the above formula – make sure you stick to it. Be logical, and only give an outline – retain the examples in your head, and include them at the most appropriate point in your answer.

Other aspects of writing extended prose:
Always keep an eye on the time. Make sure you write clearly and con-

cisely. Do not provide confused answers, or have endless sentences, or fail to paragraph.

Above all:

Read The Question and Answer The Question.

Index

ageing population 31–3, 47–8
age structure 28
assisted areas 8

balance of trade 13
Berkshire 36
birth rates 28, 31
Bournemouth 16
Bradford 53
brownfield sites 17, 41–2

call centres 14, 25
Cambridge 7, 8, 9
care in the community 47
central business district 18, 20
Central Manchester
   Development Corporation
   (CMDC) 68
city challenge partnerships 62–4,
   69
commuting 83–4, 88–9
competitiveness 4, 14, 21, 64
comprehensive community
   action programmes 58
Conservative Governments 4, 12,
   34, 58–65
Consett 5–6
Cornwall 17–18
corruption 37
council housing 34, 35–6
counter-urbanisation 57, 77,
   78–81

death rate 28
de-industrialisation 1–2, 5, 55
discrimination 50

e-commerce 20
education 45–6, 50–51, 65
education priority areas 58
enterprise zones 8, 61
ethnicity 48–51
European Union (EU) 13, 64

fertility 28

financial services 15–16
flexitime 24
footloose 7

garage shopping 20
gender issues 24, 43, 50, 51,
   73–4
general improvement areas
   (GIAs) 58
gentrification 43, 44, 72–3
government aid to industry 8
government benefits 13
Grainger Town Regeneration
   Project 69–72
green belts 77–8
greenfield sites 41–2

health care 46–7, 51, 65
homeworking 25
household composition 28,
   33–42
housing action areas 58
housing associations 34, 38–40
housing estates 36–8
housing segregation 44–5, 47–8,
   50
Hulme City Challenge 69

industrial areas (old) 2–3
industrial areas (new) 6–7
infant mortality 28, 31
inner city decline 55–8
inner city task forces 61–2
inward investment – see overseas
   investment

Just In Time (JIT) 10

Labour Governments 12, 58–9,
   65
life expectancy 28
London 3, 15, 18, 44, 83, 86,
   88–9
London Docklands 45, 61, 65–8
longevity 28

M4 Corridor 7, 10–12
Manchester 9, 16–17, 18, 21–4, 44, 68, 69, 87–8
manufacturing industry 1–14, 55–6
mass transit systems 87–8
mechanisation 2–4
Merseyside 86–7
Metrolink 22
Middlesbrough 37–8
migration 28, 31, 57
millennium schemes 65
motor vehicle industry 2–4, 7, 10, 14
multiplier effect 13

Newcastle upon Tyne 69–72
nursing homes 48

objective 1 and 2 funding 64–5
out of town shopping areas 18, 19
overseas investment 1, 2, 7, 12–14

partnerships 62–4, 69–72
pensions 31–3
pollution 85
population structure 28, 29–33
private housing 34, 36
property-led development 60–61
public transport 16

quaternary industry 15

rationalisation 4, 5
recession 4, 35
regeneration 55, 58–72
regional development agencies 65
research and development 2, 7, 8, 10, 15
retailing 1, 6, 18–24
Right to Buy legislation 34, 38, 39, 40

safety 24, 73–4

St Ives 79–81
science parks 8, 9, 12, 15, 16–17
seasonal unemployment 17
segregation
    based on age 47–8
    based on ethnicity 48–51
    based on wealth 44–7
Single Regeneration Budget (SRB) 64
social segregation 28, 42–51
self employment 25
service industry 1–2, 12, 14–25, 55–6
sheltered housing 47–8
shipbuilding 3, 6
steel industry 1–5
Stockbridge Village 39–40
subcontracting 14
suburbanisation 77–8
sunrise industries 7
Swindon 12
synergy 8, 12

technology 2, 6, 7, 10, 15, 17, 18, 25, 78
teleworking 25
tourism 15, 17–18
Trafford Centre 23–4
training and enterprise councils (TECs) 14
transfer of technology 8–10
transnationals 7, 12–14

universities 8, 10, 17
urban aid programme 58
Urban Development Corporations (UDCs) 8, 59–61, 67, 68
urban transport 83–9

waiting lists 35
working practices 4, 8–10
worksharing 24–5